Flaubert's Sentimental Education

Prepared by Arnold Kettle for the Course Team

21. 6. 79.

The Open University Press

Arnold Kettle is Professor of Literature at the Open University

The Open University Press
Walton Hall   Milton Keynes MK7 6AA

First published 1976

Designed by the Media Development Group of the Open University.

Printed in Great Britain by
EYRE AND SPOTTISWOODE
AT GROSVENOR PRESS, PORTSMOUTH

ISBN 0 335 05056 5

This text forms part of an Open University course. The complete list of units in the course appears at the end of this text.

For general availability of supporting material referred to in this text please write to the Director of Marketing, The Open University, P.O. Box 81, Walton Hall, Milton Keynes, MK7 6AT.

Further information on Open University courses may be obtained from the Admissions Office, The Open University, P.O. Box 48, Walton Hall, Milton Keynes, MK7 6AB.
1.1

CONTENTS   UNIT 13

NB   The text referred to throughout this unit is: Gustave Flaubert, *Sentimental Education*, translated by Robert Baldick, Penguin, 1964. All page references are to this edition.

Fig. 1   Gustave Flaubert
(Mansell Collection)

13.1   INTRODUCTORY

This unit assumes that you have read *Sentimental Education* in the Penguin text. There is very little point in bothering with the unit until you have read the text. But of course 'reading' or 'read' can be question-begging words. One has 'read' a book to the extent that one has understood, or – to use what may be a better phrase – come to terms with it, and this isn't something which can be measured or assessed in any simple way. But the more we realize that a text like Flaubert's is something to be coped with – thought about, read tentatively or even experimentally, looked back on and reviewed in the light of this or that new consideration or experience – the better we'll equip ourselves for coping with it. Almost all of us tend to think of reading as a simpler and more passive activity than it really ought to be.

I have ignored the question of translation and assumed that the book we are discussing is Flaubert's. It's a very big assumption and one which some scholars and critics find too big to swallow. There seems no point in rehearsing the pros and cons of the argument: it is one of those problems about which one has to take a decision and stick to it. If I didn't think Robert Baldick's translation of the novel could give us a reasonable idea of what Flaubert was doing I wouldn't be asking you to spend your time reading it.

It's a long complex novel and the time at our disposal doesn't allow us to make the deepest sort of study of it. These pages make no claim to exhaustiveness. But two double questions wend their way through them and we shall find ourselves coming back to them from different angles and in different forms:

1   What is Flaubert up to? or, what is *Sentimental Education* about?

2   In what way or ways does reading this novel tell us something about France in 1848? or, what is its value to the historian?

Part of the object of the unit is to take up some of the questions raised in the Study Guide, both in the course of the text and, specifically, in Section 4.5.3. I have not however treated these questions exhaustively: for one thing, there would not have been space, for another I don't see it as my job to provide you with a tied-up 'model answer' to all the points raised. It seems better to leave a good deal open-ended and hope you will reach conclusions of your own.

There has already been one radio programme (4) on Flaubert, in which I discuss with Professor Douglas Johnson (who is Professor of French History at University College, London) some of the interrelations between *Sentimental Education* and the purposes of an historian of the period. This programme raised some of the questions which are discussed more fully in this unit (especially in Section 13.7). If you get the chance of playing it back from a tape after you have worked on the unit it would be a good idea to do so. In the other radio programme (13), Dr Jonathan Culler (Fellow of Brasenose College, Oxford) talks about 'Sartre on Flaubert'. This talk raises – through a consideration of Sartre's book, *L'Idiot de la Famille* – a number of problems highly relevant not only to an understanding of *Sentimental Education* but to the general question of the relationship of literature to history. Sartre's approach to Flaubert is very wide-ranging and speculative; and this radio programme is, above all, one to be thought about.

13.2 SOME PRELIMINARIES

13.2.1 'SENTIMENTAL EDUCATION': WHY THAT TITLE?

Of the various possible answers (and it's unlikely there's a single one), one or two can, I think, be safely and conveniently ruled out; e.g. that this is, in the modern English sense, a 'sentimental' novel in the soppy or self-indulgent way, involving an easy and pleasurable manipulation of the reader's more easily-stirred emotions. Or that it involves an 'education' in the sense of something exemplary: a finishing school or something like that. Pretty clearly the 'education' of Frédéric and his friends isn't of the sort even the most ambitious Educational Studies faculty goes in for.

As you will recall from the Study Guide, Flaubert referred to his novel as 'the moral history of the men of my generation' and went on to say, 'It's a book about love, passion; but passion as it's bound to be now, i.e. inactive'. That added phrase reveals how easily Flaubert, in thinking about his own work, could swing over from the role of objective historian (recounting the moral history of his time) to theorizer, expressing a theory about the nature of passion nowadays. But perhaps we should give Flaubert more credit for 'scientific objectivity' – something he greatly admired – than he gives himself. I don't find, for myself, in *Sentimental Education* that I have the sense of a book being written to sustain a theory. I have, rather, the sense of a tireless effort to illuminate and define the world of a certain young man and his friends.

Where the idea of a 'sentimental education' comes in is in Flaubert's concentration on the nature of feeling and experience rather than fully formulated ideas or cut-and-dried moral assumptions. This is to be a book about the way people actually feel and behave. Not about feeling *as opposed to* thought, or sensibility *as opposed to* sense. Flaubert was certainly not one to despise rationality or to crack up feeling 'for its own sake': but he had what I think can be called a very modern attitude to human behaviour as something to probe and investigate and record rather than to categorize within accepted moral compartments. From the very opening of the novel it is clear that Frédéric's 'education' or development will not be seen in a way that isolates it from the world in which he breathes and moves. On the contrary, we are forced all the time to see Frédéric, his motives and his experiences (what might be called his 'character') in context. Indeed the 'subject' (Frédéric) and the context (the world he lives in) are inseparable. That is why there is no contradiction between Flaubert's two aims – to record the 'sentimental education' of one young man and to write 'the moral history of my generation'.

13.2.2 WHY THE 'MAN WITH LEATHER BELT'?

Gustave Courbet's picture (1844 or 1845) is right for the period and Courbet himself was very much involved with the relation between art and politics, though unlike Flaubert he became more and more revolutionary as he grew older. He was living in Paris at the time of Frédéric's adventures and joined with Baudelaire and other friends in contributing to a pro-revolutionary *feuilleton* in 1848. (See Unit 8 for illustration of cover of *Le Salut Public*.) Several of his paintings (e.g. *At the Café Andler*) have great appropriateness to the scenes of Flaubert's novel.

On the other hand there is a Romantic strength about the 'young man' which one could scarcely see in Frédéric and perhaps there is a danger of slipping into a way of seeing Courbet's young man as some kind of visual equivalent to Frédéric. T. J. Clark argues that the *Young Man* is a Romantic painting in the pejorative sense and compares it unfavourably with the great 'Bohemian' paintings which include *Man with a Pipe,* the *Café Andler* and the portrait of Baudelaire.[1] The point he is making, as I understand it, is that in the *Man with Leather Belt* there is an acceptance of a certain amount of Romantic idealization. The handsome young man is taken at his own, rather melancholy, evaluation. Whereas in the paintings Clark describes as 'Bohemian' there is a further element of self-consciousness which reflects a more mature ambiguity in Courbet's attitudes towards his subjects. Comparing a later painting with the *Man with Leather Belt,* Clark says 'he does not flex himself any longer in an effort to hold the pose'. It's not that the figures in the 'Bohemian' pictures are no longer poseurs; but rather that the attitude of the artist towards them has subtly changed. This will be clearer perhaps when we consider Bohemianism (Section 13.6). Meanwhile, if we accept Clark's view of the *Man with Leather Belt* as a Romantic picture how does it affect our sense of its appropriateness for the cover of *Sentimental Education*? I don't want to attempt a cut-and-dried answer. But I think a relevant further question for your consideration is: how does Courbet's implied attitude towards his young man compare with Flaubert's towards his?

13.3   THE WAY THE NOVEL WORKS

In this section I propose to discuss several passages from *Sentimental Education* and to try to define their importance in the novel. The object is not to say the last word about the scenes concerned but to indicate some of the ways in which Flaubert seems to operate so that you can check up as to whether you have been reading the novel with the relevant kinds of attention.

13.3.1   ROSANETTE'S FANCY-DRESS BALL (pp. 121–34)

What seems to you to be the principal point of this scene? Among the possibilities are:

(a) It tells us more about some of the chief characters.

(b) It carries forward the plot of the novel.

(c) It gives us an impression of the sort of life to which Frédéric is introduced by Arnoux.

(d) It offers a satirical description of an area of French social life.

Which of these descriptions of the scene seems to you the most appropriate?

Discussion

● Pretty clearly all four statements have *some* truth in them. We do learn more about Frédéric's acquaintances – Arnoux, Hussonet, Pellerin, Mlle Vatnaz etc. – and the episode marks a new step in Frédéric's 'education'. At first he is 'lost and ill-at-ease'. By the end of the evening, though still somewhat out of his depth, he is enjoying himself and has acquired a new thirst 'for

[1]T. J. Clark, *Image of the People,* Thames and Hudson, 1973, p. 44ff.

women, for luxury, for everything that life in Paris implies' and the impact the evening has made on him is illuminated by the extremely vivid dream with which the chapter closes.

At the same time the scene does contribute towards the development of the 'plot' of the novel – by which I mean the story-threads and other devices which provide the mechanics of the book, holding it together and making it work. Rosanette, for instance, is to play a major role in the book and therefore it's important that she should be effectively introduced into it. The little intrigue around old Oudry (whom we have already met as a neighbour of the Arnoux at Saint-Cloud) is another example of 'carrying the plot forward', for he is to play a continuing, though subsidiary, part in Rosanette's fortunes.

At the same time, Flaubert's description has a kind of 'documentary' quality about it. We are given a glimpse of the *demi-monde* of Paris of the forties: a world far less rich and exotic (as Flaubert himself remarks later) than that of the Second Empire, but sufficiently in contrast to the world of Nogent. The way Flaubert dodges about from figure to figure, evoking clothes, meetings, snatches of conversation etc., clearly indicates his interest in the scene as such, as a social phenomenon, significant in quite other ways (more *generalized* ways perhaps) than as a simple following-up of the story of certain individuals. The personal narrative in a passage like this expands into a social documentary. Episodes like the 'Sphinx's' illness have no *direct* bearing on Frédéric's or Rosanette's story, but they contribute significantly to the total effect of the scene and of the novel as a whole. Rosanette's dealings with Delmar and with Oudry (who is presumably in the bedroom when Rosanette slams the door in the Sphinx's face) are important less for any personal significance they may have than as factors in a way of life.

But satire? Well, certainly the scene Flaubert presents us with is not described without critical implications. The nightmare at the end forces the reader to look back on the party in a particular way, even if he wasn't exercising his judgment already. Yet if Flaubert is making a general satirical comment about this particular area of Parisian society he isn't doing it in the ways one most often associates with satire. The reader doesn't, I think, see the people *primarily* as exhibits, though obviously they have something of that aspect and are chosen for (among other things) a certain quality of representativeness. But though the scene is obviously 'pointed' (i.e. Flaubert directs our attention to selected emphases), the satirical implications seem to me to be always contained within the essentially 'realistic' convention of the novel. A good example is the fine moment on p. 125 when Pellerin is giving Frédéric the low-down on some of the people at the party and describes Captain Herbigny. Frédéric's reaction 'A scoundrel?' is capped by Pellerin's 'No, a decent fellow'. 'Oh!' says Frédéric and the exclamation is at the same time the expression of a new stage in his education and an authorial comment full of ironical implication. Yet whatever its more general implications the passage as a whole remains, I think, an account of what Frédéric and his friends actually do and say and think.●

13.3.2 FRÉDÉRIC'S LUNCHEON PARTY (pp. 141–7)

This is another 'public' scene in the sense that a number of characters are brought together and the general effect goes beyond the revelation of certain personal relationships: the scene enhances the reader's sense of the socio-historical situation within which Frédéric lives. One can't, I think, avoid feeling that Frédéric's friends are in some sense 'representatives' – embodying in their interests and personalities a number of significant trends in the social and intellectual life of the time. Hussonet, Pellerin and the absent Arnoux take us into the world of art; Deslauriers, Sénécal and Dussardier are three different sorts of 'politically-conscious' individuals; Cisy is the would-be trendy aristocrat, just as Martinon (who, significantly, is *not* invited) is the would-be bourgeois.

The questions arise: (a) How far does Flaubert succeed in combining the *personal* (i.e. the presentation of individualized characters) with the *representative* (i.e. the convincing portrayal of trends or tendencies in public and intellectual life)? and (b) How 'objective' is his presentation? Make notes on these questions before you go further.

Discussion

● My own response to (a) is that the characters are convincing as individuals but that one has the quite definite sense that their *primary* significance within the pattern of the novel (at least as far as this scene is concerned) is as representatives or types, not so much of social or intellectual trends as such (i.e. in the way a social historian might list such trends), as of those forces which most affect the development of a young man like Frédéric in his given situation. The very fact that they are all so different enforces this response: one gets an insistent sense of Frédéric's friends having been in some way 'chosen'. But perhaps it is Frédéric who has indeed chosen them because each embodies some facet of his needs or aspiration. So there isn't necessarily a contradiction between the 'individual' and the 'representative' any more than one can make a valid distinction between Frédéric's personal taste and those of the time. That they have in their way something to do with the development of French imperial ambitions of the period is left for the reader to infer.

(b) The question of the 'objectivity' of Flaubert's presentation of the scene is rather complex. As far as the characters are concerned it's not, you may feel, quite appropriate to use the word 'objective' at all, since they are Flaubert's own creations and there can be no outside 'objective' criterion against which one can test them. Yet one can sometimes have the sense that a novelist doesn't play quite fair with his characters and presents some of them with a certain animus which arouses the reader's suspicions. Is this true perhaps of the presentation of Sénécal? It's not that one doubts that someone like him – doctrinaire and self-deceiving – could exist. But, just because he is presented as in some way a *representative* character standing for, if not socialists in general, at least a type of socialist, one does, I think, suspect Flaubert's intentions. To dismiss 'the whole cartload of Socialist writers' (including Fourier, Saint-Simon and Comte) as 'those who wanted to reduce mankind to the level of the barrack-room, send it to the brothel for amusement, and tie it to the counter or the bench' will seem to most readers – whatever their personal views – to be a good deal short of reasonably objective: and since it's in this context that Sénécal is presented it seems fair to accuse Flaubert of stacking the cards.

How much does this matter? The whole question of Flaubert's personal bias is discussed in Section 13.7. If you argue that Flaubert's animus against socialism makes his total presentation of Sénécal less than convincing, you have then to consider the contrary argument that the open disclosure of that bias at once puts the reader on his guard and allows him to discount it. After all, this contrary argument will run, every writer has certain prejudices embodied in his point of view; sometimes it is the very quality of those prejudices which provides the individual tone and insight one values in a work of art (one doesn't reject Milton because he is a Christian or Gibbon because he isn't). Is it not a part of the total effect of *Sentimental Education* that it should embody a view of the situation it is evoking which – right or wrong – is an integral part of the book and can no more be wished away than the unbalanced towers of Chartres cathedral or the final movement of Vaughan Williams' sixth symphony?●

13.3.3   THE FONTAINEBLEAU EPISODE (pp. 318–29)

A full analysis of this passage would take us further into a discussion of Flaubert's style than we have time for – especially as we are reading the book in translation. Nevertheless the episode is so striking an example of the way Flaubert works that it seems sensible to look at some of the more obvious problems it raises.

What part does the episode play in the structure of the novel?

Discussion

● Frédéric takes Rosanette off to Fontainebleau as the situation in Paris moves towards a new stage (the June Days). On the previous page (p. 317) is the striking image of the working men surging along the boulevard as an elemental force. It is one of the recurring patterns of the novel that the turns or developments in Frédéric's life should be linked, if only by a kind of counterpoint, with the public developments. The Fontainebleau episode has to be seen within the total narrative-structure of *Sentimental Education*, that is to say between the events in Paris leading up to the June Days and those to which Frédéric returns, to find Dussardier wounded and old Roque firing into the Tuileries.

Is it simply a contrast – a sort of rural idyll – sandwiched between scenes of social unrest? To interpret it this way (as some critics have) seems somewhat naïve. Contrast there certainly is, but isn't the idyll altogether too shoddy to be taken quite seriously? Frédéric and Rosanette react differently to Fontainebleau and its charms but in each case the reaction tells us more about his or her brand of escapism than about anything else. To see the episode as a charming romantic dream throwing into contrast the sordid reality of what is happening in Paris seems to be taking the whole thing rather too much on Frédéric's own evaluation – an evaluation which itself breaks down rather quickly when faced with the fact of Dussardier's danger.

It's easy enough to recognize that Rosanette's responses to Fontainebleau are trivial and frivolous. She is more interested in 'souvenirs' than in scenery, in teasing Frédéric than in understanding Diane de Poitiers. But are Frédéric's own responses much more serious? Romantic history and the 'beauties of nature' are his line. His brand of tourism is a bit more sophisticated than Rosanette's, but is it really more 'serious', if 'seriousness' has anything to do with the situation? It's true that *Flaubert* (as opposed to his characters) builds up an episode that is visually and atmospherically marvellously effective, but surely those critics who refuse to see anything deeply symbolic in his presenta-

10

tion of the forest are right? What do you make of a passage like this?

> They thought that they were far from other people, completely alone. But all of a sudden a gamekeeper would go by with his gun, or a band of women in rags dragging along great bundles of faggots on their backs.

> When the carriage stopped there was complete silence; all that could be heard was the breathing of the horse in the shafts, or the faint, repeated cry of a bird. (p. 322)

I suppose it is possible to see the gamekeeper as a 'symbol' of the old order and the women in rags as 'representing' the poor whom the lovers have run away from. But to put it this way seems a bit heavy-handed. Certainly the women with their burdens are reminders (to the reader if not to Frédéric and Rosanette) of a world 'beneath' the beauties of Fontainebleau, but the passage works through the evocation of actual physical impressions and reactions rather than through processes that it seems right to call 'symbolic' in the cruder sense.

It's certainly significant that it is in this atmosphere that Rosanette tells Frédéric about her youth and the whole sordid story of her 'ruin'. When I describe Rosanette's reactions to Fontainebleau as 'frivolous' I'm aware that in one sense this is an inadequate word. She is, it can well be argued, more honest than Frédéric (the phrase 'retrospective lust' (p. 320) tells us a lot about him) and has, at the same time, more excuse for wanting to 'escape from' realities. It's interesting that, though Frédéric likes from time to time to persuade himself that 'the people are sublime' and that he is profoundly devoted to them, it is Rosanette who is really a woman of the people; and I would say that on the whole the Fontainebleau episode increases the reader's sympathy for her despite the triviality and selfishness of her reactions, making us see her vulgarity – and indeed 'vulgarity' as such – rather differently.

The role of Fontainebleau in developing the 'story' of the novel – Frédéric's relationship with Rosanette – and in foreshadowing his loss of interest in her (he is about to transfer his attention to Mme Dambreuse) only makes sense, however, if one also recognizes its role as an *image* within the total structure of the book. These pages, coming between the description of the February days (pp. 285–94) and that of the bourgeois world epitomized by the Dambreuses' salon (pp. 336–49), are an essential part of Flaubert's revelation of Frédéric's reactions to and relationship with the Revolution of 1848. Mme Arnoux has, he believes, let him down. He turns to Rosanette as the people of Paris march through the streets. He shares the optimism of his friends like Dussardier about the revolution. Then, as the crisis of July develops, he goes off with Rosanette to Fontainebleau, coming back because his conscience is stirred by the news of Dussardier. Yet the chapter ends not with Frédéric or Rosanette or Dussardier, but with old Roque shooting down the rebels in the Tuileries and his daughter realizing that her own image of Frédéric is false. Flaubert's way is not the way of the simple narrative story-teller. He works through a complex series of blocks and images, narrative passages and more or less 'symbolic' moments. And it is through the total complexity that he gets his effects and we get our sense of what his novel is offering.

13.3.4 THE LAST CHAPTER

What would you consider its principal purpose: (a) to round off the story and tell us what becomes of the characters? (b) to sum up Frédéric's education? (c) to stress a special tone or note?

Discussion

● Fairly obviously it does all three: but (a) seems to me much less important than (b) or (c).

Frédéric's and Deslauriers' 'story' *qua* story could end logically enough before or after this, and we are only marginally interested in the events in the lives of them and their friends *per se*. The central question embedded in the sentences 'They had both failed . . . What was the reason?' is more important than the bits of information about their friends etc. And it is a question they are unable to answer, at least in direct terms.

It seems answered however in indirect terms by the final anecdote of the novel: their recollection of their abortive visit to the brothel. As we often find in our discussion of *Sentimental Education*, it isn't easy to put into other words the meaning or significance or status of this final anecdote. Enid Starkie is one of those who have tried:

> This ending has been severely criticized as cynical and immoral, and frequently misunderstood. It has been thought that Flaubert was saying that their best moment had been when, as children, they had gone to the brothel. That was not however what Flaubert intended to say. On the contrary, he was saying that the best moment in their life had been when they had *not* carried out what they had planned. One of Flaubert's strongest beliefs was that happiness and fulfilment consist in anticipation and not in realization. The two youths had been frustrated in their attempt to reach sexual experience with the prostitutes, and so had not been disappointed or disillusioned. He believed that fulfilment cheapens aspiration. (Enid Starkie, *Flaubert the Master*, Weidenfeld and Nicolson, 1971, p. 176.)

Enid Starkie is certainly right in saying that anyone is wrong who thinks the passage implies that the two men's best moment had really consisted in going to the brothel. Whether her own view is correct, however, seems less certain for it suggests that Flaubert is identifying with Frédéric more than he does. It seems more likely that the 'that' referred to[2] is the time of their youth and innocence in general rather than their specific conduct in the brothel. But perhaps even that is tying down the meaning too tightly. The effect of the little episode, placed where it is, is above all to deflate. It is the final deflationary act of a novel whose continuous effort is to undermine the romantic, the pretentious and the crudely moralistic.●

13.4 FRÉDÉRIC MOREAU

13.4.1 HIS 'CHARACTER'

Let us avoid dividing the question (as literary critics sometimes do) into two: 'What is Frédéric like?' and 'What is Flaubert's attitude towards him?' For we know and can know nothing of Frédéric save what Flaubert tells us and what he tells us subsumes his attitude. Frédéric is a character in fiction and exists only in so far as the novelist gives him life through the words he offers us. So that we *cannot* think of Frédéric except in terms of Flaubert's attitudes which determine the choice of words through which he is presented to us.

---

[2] '*c'est là*' is the (repeated) phrase in the original.

Let us also avoid, as far as we can, separating Frédéric from the rest of the book and discussing him as a 'character' who has some sort of existence apart from what he does in the book. It is true that, like all successful novelists, Flaubert manages to give Frédéric a vitality which makes us feel that he is 'really' there and allows us to speculate about him in the way we speculate about people we meet in actual life. But unless our speculation is based only on the actual evidence – Flaubert's words – it will be irrelevant.

Frédéric is, when we first see him, a provincial young man with Romantic aspirations and no very clear sense about where he is actually going. He knows he needs money to get away from Nogent and his mother and he feels little but dislike for provincial life.[3] But his aspirations have little basis in reality. They are more like daydreams. Yet to say that is not, of course, to dismiss them as without interest. Daydreams are as significant elements in life as what we generally think of as 'facts'. You see a young man sitting gazing out of the window on a bus from Leeds to Manchester. Are the 'facts' that the bus is going from Leeds to Manchester and crossing the Pennines at so many miles an hour 'really' more important than what the young man is thinking about, or what he notices as he sits there and why? What we learn about Frédéric in the first chapter of the novel (see Study Guide pp. 21ff.) is not simply or *chiefly* that he is travelling on a certain day from Paris to Nogent or even that he meets the Arnoux. It is, I think you're bound to agree, more importantly an introduction to what Frédéric is 'like', which is bound up with what his life (his relationships with the outside world) is like. How does Flaubert let us know what Frédéric is 'like'?

Discussion

● (a) By placing him in a situation (after all none of us is ever out of a situation, a context) which in one sense exists irrespective of him but which his presence makes a difference to. We see Frédéric in relation to the boat, the landscape, the other people around: and we see *them* in relation to him. Not necessarily (though sometimes) through his eyes, *always* through Flaubert's, though a factor in the situation is that we are aware, at some level or other, that Flaubert too is not without his context. He is no more 'absolute' than Frédéric or the Seine or the Romantic ideas that fill Frédéric's mind and colour, perhaps even determine, what he sees. As the final chapter reminds us, the novel is written in 1867 and therefore distances by twenty years or so all it evokes.

(b) The method Flaubert uses in composing his text is not at all simple and I shall not attempt, especially at this stage, to give a full account of it, though I hope a reasonably full one will emerge from the unit as a whole. But certain important elements of that method are worth stressing :

(i) The visual element (description or evocation) is very important: the novel is rather like a film.

(ii) The problematic element: Flaubert often leaves us guessing as to how Frédéric's reactions to something are to be taken. He wants to be an artist, a writer: how seriously are we to take his aspirations? The most usual way of getting this effect is simply to record Frédéric's reactions ('Frédéric thought

---

[3]I shan't have space to take up this point but it is surely a significant fact that Frédéric considers life anywhere but in Paris intolerable. The difficulty of French intellectuals in living anywhere but in Paris is a striking feature of modern French life.

that . . . ', 'He was of the opinion that . . . ' etc) without comment. Flaubert himself, in other words, is not necessarily underwriting Frédéric's own thoughts. Sometimes he specifically dissociates himself from Frédéric by a comment (explicit or implicit) which expresses contempt or criticism. But most of the time he leaves the reader to draw his own conclusions by evaluating Frédéric's reactions on the basis of the knowledge he has gained from the overall impressions which the book makes, and indeed from his knowledge of life in general.

(iii) The 'symbolic' element: scenes, episodes, phrases in the book quite often have a force or value beyond that of straightforward, self-justifying description. One can describe this force as 'symbolic' as long as one isn't implying that the surface meaning simply 'stands for' something else in the way that, for instance, the sign ☺ has come to be a 'symbol' of the Open University. If one says that Frédéric's and Deslauriers' visit to the 'Turkish' brothel, described in the final chapters but hinted at more than once during the narrative, is 'symbolic', what one means isn't that it 'stands for' something other than itself, but that it has within the overall pattern or structure of the book a significance which surpasses the relatively casual empirical significance of the single fact or action. This particular episode gives us a special kind of insight into recurring 'patterns' within Frédéric's life (see above pp. 10–11) and therefore helps shape the book for us in the way a repeated (or slightly varied) musical phrase can give us a sense of the structure or 'argument' of a piece of music, or a spotlight can illuminate not just the figure on the stage upon which it's directed, but the whole significance of the scene being enacted. The spotlight is perhaps an over-simple example of 'symbolic' significance since what it provides is usually just a form of emphasis, whereas a 'symbolic' episode like the two boys' visit to the brothel gains its effect in a much subtler way, hinting at patterns of behaviour and forms of illusion buried fairly deep in the situations the novelist is exploring.●

Are we supposed to sympathize with Frédéric?

Discussion

● Though you may feel that this is obvious, I feel it's important to emphasize that Flaubert is not asking us to 'identify' with Frédéric or to take him uncritically. Many readers who become impatient with *Sentimental Education* do so either because they feel (without perhaps being quite conscious of it) that the main character in a novel *ought* to be a hero in the more conventional sense of the term (i.e. someone you can admire) or because they think Flaubert expects them to like Frédéric better than they do. I don't think there can be any question of Frédéric's being a hero in the everyday sense of the word. By no conceivable standards (his own, those of the class to which he belongs, Flaubert's) is he either admirable or successful. You might even say that his major achievement is not to finish up worse, or worse off, than he actually is. He neither achieves anything much nor enjoys himself much except for rather short spaces of time. There is scarcely a character in the book towards whom he behaves other than badly. Does this mean that we feel no sort of sympathy for him?

Well, that depends, of course, on *us*. My reason for asking the question is not to get you to award yourself some grade between R and A for compassion; but rather to ask you to consider whether, as it's put, it's quite the right question. Is 'sympathy' necessarily a commodity we ought to be stressing in discussing this novel? Isn't comprehension or understanding perhaps more relevant?

14

One may argue, of course, that any deep understanding of some area of human experience involves in some way an extension of one's human sympathies, or even that 'to understand all is to pardon all'. But I'm not sure myself that the reader is really called upon to 'pardon' the characters in a work of fiction and I very much doubt if Flaubert would have had much sympathy for such an idea. More to the point perhaps are some remarks of Peter Cortland:

> The author (of *Sentimental Education*) is exploring the contradictions, the glories and the debacles of the world of sentimentality, and in doing so is asking the reader for a greater degree of self-analysis, of a particularly deflating sort, than the latter is usually prepared to attempt. The novel is not so much about Frédéric Moreau as it is about the reader's perceptions, and a study of the novel must assess the latter's reaction to the work . . . (Peter Cortland, *The Sentimental Adventure*, Mouton, 1967, p. 8.)

In other words, in reading *Sentimental Education* we have to be constantly evaluating what is happening and this involves us in a consideration not so much of Frédéric's psychology or character in the abstract as of Frédéric's *situation*, which is an historical situation, and of our own relationship to that situation which is, at least to some extent, an historical matter too. ●

Two of the main elements in Frédéric's situation are his relationship with (a) Deslauriers and (b) Mme Arnoux.

13.4.2   FRÉDÉRIC AND DESLAURIERS

Frédéric's relationship with Deslauriers is more complex and important than his relationship with anyone else in the novel except perhaps Mme Arnoux. It is important that Deslauriers should be the first of his friends to appear in the novel (at the end of Chapter 1) and the last too. Deslauriers has, one might say, a key *structural* part in the book: he is an essential element in the presentation of Frédéric himself. It's not that the two men even like one another particularly. On the contrary they behave extremely badly to one another: yet in some strange way they are bound to one another 'by that irresistible element in their nature which always united them in friendship' (p. 416). Those 'we' in the last sentences of the book unite them in some (fictionally) organic way.[4]

What is it that links them so strongly?

Discussion

● The links that one might describe as plot-links aren't really the main thing. These are that both come from Nogent, that they were at school together, that Deslauriers lives with Frédéric in Paris, that they are both involved with the Dambreuses and, latterly, with the Arnoux, Rosanette and finally, Louise Roque. I call these 'plot-links' because although important in the manipulative procedures of the novel they don't quite explain the peculiar closeness of the relationship and indeed tend to stretch it to breaking-point, as

---

[4]Note: Flaubert goes out of his way to make clear there is no homosexuality involved: even in Frédéric's first small apartment they do not share a room.

when Deslauriers, trying to seduce Mme Arnoux, falsely tells her that Frédéric is married and when he himself marries Louise. On a succession of occasions, indeed, they behave so badly towards one another that it is quite hard to understand why either should ever want to see the other again. Yet they do.

The link therefore, must have some basis different from the relatively casual personal relationship Frédéric has with his other friends, even Dussardier. It is a link more comparable to the sort of affinity Frédéric feels for Mme Arnoux.

I think that one way of defining the significance of the relationship is to suggest that Frédéric and Deslauriers share many of the problems, needs and characteristics of their class but are also separated by a key difference: Frédéric is a Romantic; Deslauriers is not.

In one sense the two young men represent the opposite sides of the same coin. They are nearly the same age, come from the same part of the country, and are both products of the post-Revolutionary (1789) provincial middle class or, more accurately, petty bourgeoisie. But because Frédéric is better-off than his friend he is able to indulge himself in a kind of day-dreaming that Deslauriers can never quite afford. Deslauriers is at the same time ambitious, radical and prepared to make any compromise that happens to suit him. Like most opportunists, he can always find principles to throw around, but the driving-force of his life is personal ambition of a kind characteristic of the petty bourgeoisie: he wants to 'rise' socially while retaining a contempt for those higher in the social scale whom he is quite prepared to use for his purposes. But he isn't really a very effective go-getter.

Frédéric for all his inheritance of wealth and kow-towing with the Dambreuse set, is every bit as petty-bourgeois as Deslauriers. He kids himself that he sympathizes with the revolution and has aspirations to being a deputy (member of parliament): in a way he is 'sincere' or 'genuine' enough in his radical sympathies – as long as you don't test them against his actions or expect any high measure of consistency. Deslauriers, urged on by the necessity of earning a living (though he is happy enough to sponge on Frédéric much of the time), is forced into rather more action and at one point even suffers (or persuades himself he does) for his republican convictions. But as we look back on the novel – and the final chapter reinforces this – it's hard to choose between the two of them as far as effectiveness or 'success' goes. What Flaubert seems to be illuminating are the two sides of the petty-bourgeois intellectual – the 'middle-class' young man who is neither a bourgeois nor a worker but 'uses' both bourgeois and workers to provide him with the wherewithal to pursue his baseless and ineffectual dreams.

For one way of seeing the roles of Frédéric-Deslauriers in the novel is to note how in these two petty-bourgeois young men sensibility (Frédéric's forte) and power (what Deslauriers is after) are separated. The two young men from Nogent confront their destiny and neither makes much of it. Frédéric's development centres on his romantic aspirations, embodied in his feeling for Mme Arnoux: Deslauriers' on his desire to 'get on'. Frédéric is the dreamer, Deslauriers the 'realist'. Frédéric is able to dream because he has money; Deslauriers has to be more cynical in order to have enough to live on. But both are trapped within the social limitations and, especially, the ideology of their class. And their youthful, ineffectual adventure in the 'Turk's' brothel is indeed an illumination of their life. They like to persuade themselves that they were too good for this world, that somehow they have lost an innocence they might have retained. But neither of them from the start to the finish of the novel reveals the remotest idea of what might have gone wrong. Nor does

Flaubert hand us the moral neatly inscribed on a platter. He hands us his novel, four hundred pages long.●

13.4.3   THE CRITIQUE OF ROMANTICISM: FRÉDÉRIC AND MADAME ARNOUX

Frédéric inherits (historically, not of course through heredity) some of the main ideas and attitudes of Romanticism. What do I mean by this? Give some examples.

Discussion

●   To take some examples first:

1   Descriptions of Frédéric in Chapter 1 (especially p. 16). See also the Study Guide, pp. 24–5.

2   He is attracted by Mme Arnoux who 'looked like the women in romantic novels' (p. 22).

3   The literary characters who influence him are all from Romantic literature: Werther, René, etc. (p. 27 and note 2, p. 420).

4   A particularly rich passage on p. 78 (especially paragraph beginning 'When he went to the Jardin des Plantes . . .') brings in all the paraphernalia of late Romanticism in describing Frédéric's feelings.

5   His Romantic view of the February revolution (e.g. p. 292).

You will no doubt have found many others.●

Romanticism as a movement or tendency is mentioned explicitly as well as implicitly many times in the book. Have you noticed such references?

Discussion

●   For instance:

1   Hussonet attacks Romantic poets (p. 44). The attack is frivolous and demonstrates (among other things) the hollowness of some current *anti*-Romantic modishness.

2   Pellerin's changing views on art (pp. 47 ff.).

3   The role of Lamartine, a leading Romantic poet, in the revolution.●

But if Frédéric is deeply impregnated with Romantic ideas and Flaubert himself highly conscious of Romanticism as a phenomenon, this does not imply that *Sentimental Education* is a Romantic novel. Quite the contrary: Flaubert's attitude to Romanticism, both as an historical phenomenon and as a literary movement with certain implications for any writer of his time, was highly critical. He regarded himself as a realist, an objective, even scientific, artist committed not to Romantic ideas but to Art itself. The tendency of the Romantic artist to pour out his own, more or less unmediated, feelings into his art and to identify in some basic way with revolutionary aspiration, was antipathetic to him. Romantic attitudes were to him essentially delusions and his novel is both a critique of Romanticism and – in its own technique and

17

Fig. 2   *Lamartine addresses the crowd at the Hôtel de Ville, 26 February 1848. (Bibliothèque Nationale)*

spirit – an *alternative* to Romanticism: aloof, ironical, sceptical. Between Flaubert's view of objectivity, which involved a sense of the *supremacy* (not to say superiority) of the artist and that of, say, a Romantic like Wordsworth, seeking to record his sense of *unity* with the world of nature and mankind, there is a very deep gap. As Dr Culler puts it in his radio lecture describing Sartre's view of Flaubert: 'this (i.e. Flaubert's) generation's feeling of *ennui* or *mal du siècle* came not from Romanticism itself but from the fact that romantic roles and postures were no longer open to them'. I will return to this point in comparing Flaubert's novel with Stendhal's *Scarlet and Black*.

Meanwhile Flaubert's critique of Romanticism in *Sentimental Education* is, clearly, centred on his presentation of the relationship of Frédéric and Madame Arnoux. What have you made of this relationship and the value the reader is expected to give it? (i.e. Do you think for instance that Flaubert wants us to feel sympathetic to the couple in the way Shakespeare pretty clearly assumes sympathy for Romeo and Juliet? If not, then how would you define his attitude?)

1   What are the chief characteristics of the relationship?
2   Why does one use the word Romantic about it?
3   And what are its chief implications as far as the essential meaning of Flaubert's novel is concerned?

Let us take each question separately. Please jot down notes of your own towards an answer.

Discussion

● 1   *The chief characteristics of the Frédéric-Madame Arnoux relationship.*

Without attempting to list them in an order of priority some of them are:

It is unhappy yet in some way deeply enjoyable to both parties.
It is unconsummated.
There is throughout a strong element of idealization.
It is all very vague and subject to all manner of misunderstandings.
It involves on both sides an aspiration towards something 'better' than is settled for by most of the other people in the novel.
There is a 'mother-son' aspect to it.
It implies a criticism, even a rejection, of the values – money-making, posses-siveness (coupled with a hypocritical sentimentality) – of most of Frédéric's and the Arnoux' circle: at the same time there is little connection between the feelings of the lovers and any actual actions they take.

There is (isn't there?) something both rather admirable and more than a bit ridiculous about the relationship, an ambiguity marvellously well caught in the penultimate chapter of the novel (pp. 411ff.) in which idealization, absurdity, lost opportunities and a sense that unfulfilment is the essence of the situation, all mix. This chapter is both touching and deflating. When Marie asks him if he will ever marry and he says he won't because of her, we know it is both untrue and true. He may well marry; but he is not just being kind. She (or his image of her) *has* deeply influenced his life and the relationship *has* in a sense involved the best of him. Again, the reference (p. 415) to 'an indefinable feeling, a repugnance akin to a dread of committing incest' is significant. Mme Arnoux is very much of a mother-figure for Frédéric, a fantasy-version of what he would have liked his own mother to have been (in this as in other respects she contrasts interestingly with Rosanette and his ambiguous feelings about *her* motherhood). That final scene between Frédéric and Mme Arnoux exemplifies the nature of the novel as a whole: it is about a sentimental situation, but it is not sentimental in its treatment of that situation.

2   *Why does one use the word Romantic?*

The relationship is Romantic in the sense that it involves genuine aspiration, a genuine stretching out of two human beings towards new frontiers, new dimensions, a relationship more fully humane than the dominant structures of feeling and social norms of their time easily permit. It is Romantic in the sense of being an alternative to the cynical 'realism' of conventional bourgeois morality as exemplified in so much of the behaviour the novel recounts. It is Romantic in the sense of glimpsing new possibilities in the way of individual freedom and development. But it is also romantic in a pejorative sense, for it involves a great deal of self-deception, idealization and unrealism. Above all it involves an idealization of unfulfilment. In an important sense, we can't help feeling the relationship only lasts as something 'beautiful' *because* it isn't con-summated. The apparent chance that prevents Marie Arnoux from keeping her assignation with Frédéric in June 1848 is really, we feel, more than a chance. She *has* to fail him: the deepest need of their relationship is that it should remain idealized rather than have to come to terms with realities. So that when I call it an 'alternative' to conventional bourgeois values it isn't much of an alternative since its values are given little embodiment in action. The lack of consummation isn't just a sexual matter but a failure to discover a way of life which bears some secure relation to the values the lovers' feelings seek to embody.

3 Implications

I don't think there can be much doubt that one of the main themes of *Sentimental Education* is the demonstration that Romantic ideas are of little use to Frédéric in his 'education' and that, whatever may have been their value as a liberating force for an earlier generation, by 1848 (and certainly by 1867) they hinder rather than assist any serious response to the issues of the day. We are back, in fact, to Flaubert's insistence that 'the moral history of the men of his generation' was inevitably a depressing one. Romanticism, once a vigorous assertion of the aspirations of men and women seeking a better life, has become in practice a form of escape and self-deception. Because the young men of Frédéric's generation have failed to link themselves up with any forward-going, humanly progressive movement in history (as the first Romantics linked themselves with the Revolution of 1789), Romanticism has degenerated into a self-indulgent sentimentalism.

Why has this happened? It is not Flaubert's way to offer us theories or speculations. His method is to assert. He offers us not a theory about Romanticism but a work of art which, through its power to convince us of its own authenticity, shows us what is true. If you call it an *interpretation* of the life of his time you use the word in the sense not of an argued, speculative critique, but in the sense that a painter will offer a portrait as in some way truer of his subject that anyone has seen before. In other words he doesn't start with a theory about Romanticism and proceed to 'illustrate' it: he starts with the situation of Frédéric Moreau and explores that, creating his novel.

If we are to draw conclusions from *Sentimental Education* about the development and significance of Romanticism as an intellectual force in nineteenth-century France, then our evidence has to be (it's the crux of Flaubert's theory of art) the novel itself. If the novel 'works' (i.e. succeeds as art), then what it 'says' is true: otherwise it would not work.●

13.5 PRIVATE AND PUBLIC

Among the questions I posed at the end of the Study Guide is this one:

> Some critics have felt that there is little or no connection between the 'historical background' and the personal story, love affairs etc. of Frédéric and the other characters . . . What sort of connections do you see between the 'public' and 'private' aspects of the novel?[5]

Please jot down some notes towards an answer to this question.

Discussion
● The question has, I hope, been partly answered in Section 13.3, particularly in the discussion of the Fontainebleau episode. But a more general

[5]NB   An example of the sort of criticism I'm referring to is the passage from Martin Turnell's *The Novel in France* quoted in the Study Guide, pp. 17–18.

consideration is needed. You will have gathered that I do not myself agree with the criticism and think that Zola was right in describing *Sentimental Education* as a truly historical novel (Study Guide, p. 20). One's approach to this question is, of course, to some extent bound up with what one feels an 'historical novel' ought to be. For the purposes of this discussion I am assuming that a truly historical novel is one which (among other things) does indeed reveal interesting connections between the private or personal lives and feelings of the characters and the general situation, seen historically, within which they operate.

Now no-one, I take it, will want to argue that there is *no* connection between Frédéric's 'private' life and amours and the public events of 1840–51 which are referred to in the novel. But many readers undoubtedly feel that such connections as there are are pretty tenuous. What has Frédéric's romantic idealization of Mme Arnoux to do with the 1848 revolution? Isn't the behaviour of most of the people in the book due to their personal 'characters', virtues or vices rather than to their historical situation? Is there really anything 'symbolic' (and therefore, perhaps, related to wider developments) about the death of Monsieur Dambreuse or the hysterical exhaustion of old Roque after he has added his shot in the massacre in the Tuileries?

The question is a tricky one because it is clear that Flaubert did not think that there were obvious, easily definable connections of a crudely deterministic kind between the way his people behave and the historical forces which affect them. He *does* suggest that there's a definite connection between money – or economic security – and the way people behave. Frédéric's fortune plays no small part in determining his opportunities to live (and think and feel) in a particular way. The crowd at the Dambreuses' salon behave (and think and feel) the way they do because they have in common certain characteristics and interests as a *class* which strongly predispose them to be hostile to the revolution when it is threatening their privileges. The fact that Dussardier behaves (and thinks and feels) as he does is certainly not unconnected with the fact that he is a worker who lives by his own labour and is not involved in the various 'get-rich-quick' schemes of most of Frédéric's circle. All this is quite basic to the view of the world Flaubert is expressing. Yet he doesn't, of course, imply that there is some inevitable, measurable relationship between the details of each individual's personality and his precise social position. And if he did imply such a thing a critic like Martin Turnell would justifiably accuse him of grossly over-simplifying things.

The connections between the moral or sentimental history of the men of his generation, which it was Flaubert's object to record, and the general socio-political history of the time are certainly not presented in a crude over-simplified way. And for this reason it is quite easy for people who don't get hold of Flaubert's method, and therefore read the book imperceptively, to miss them altogether. But it is the basis of the whole argument of this unit that the connections are not merely there but are fundamental to the whole intention, meaning and value of the book.

Let us take two examples, connected with the underlying structure of the novel:

(a) The first two parts of the novel are concerned with the world of the pre-1848 July Monarchy, a world presented as, above all, corrupt and money-centred. It is Frédéric's inheritance that gives him access to the 'Establishment' which dominates that world. Without money he would probably have had to follow his mother's advice and live a provincial life based on Nogent: his career would inevitably have become more like Deslauriers'. Just as it is money that enables Arnoux, at least for a time, to indulge himself in Rosanette's *demi-monde*, so it is money that enables Frédéric to indulge his romantic obsession with Mme Arnoux in the particular way he does. What the first two parts of the novel are 'about' is – I would want to argue – precisely the connections between the nature of French society in the 1840s and the personal values, emotions, eccentricities, dreams and 'way of life' of the individuals Flaubert presents to us. These individuals are not presented *simply* as 'products' of the world of the July Monarchy: but none is presented as essentially unaffected by that world. None of them 'rises above' the social world in which he lives and it is the implication of Flaubert's treatment of his people and of his whole literary method that they are indeed *unable* to do anything of the kind. Those who attempt to do so – like Frédéric himself through his '*grande passion*' for Mme Arnoux – are merely deceiving themselves: and their illusions (you might call it 'false consciousness') are themselves a part of the total social situation the novel reveals. Sénécal becomes an agent of the state he has affected to despise, not *in spite* of being a socialist, but *because* he is a socialist of a mechanistic, doctrinaire and bogus kind (as has already been indicated by his role when he works for Arnoux). Hussonet's eccentricities are bound up, not with some abstract notion of eccentricity as a type of character, but with his ability to jump on one cultural band-wagon after another, each a part of a social trend more basic than his 'character'. Trendy as he is, it is not he who produces the trends, any more than Pellerin's changing philosophies of art spring out of some personal inner logic unconnected with the changing conditions the revolution throws up.

There is an interesting passage near the very beginning of *L'Idiot de la Famille* in which Sartre, settling down to his consideration of Flaubert and his art, tries to define the relationship between the individual and the totality, man and society: 'A man is never an individual simply: it would be better to call him a *singular universal*. Totalized and at the same time universalized by the epoch he lives in, he retotalizes it in achieving himself within it as something unique.'[6] It is a difficult sentence and difficult to translate: but I think that Sartre, with his insistence that a man must be seen and studied simultaneously as something unique and as a part of a totality, is trying to tackle the very problem that most absorbed Flaubert. It is indeed the capacity of Flaubert's style to unite the 'singular' and the 'universal' that so attracts Sartre despite his hostility to the whole project of '*l'art pour l'art*'. And it is in so far as we are able to comprehend and define this dialectical relationship between the individual and the totality that we shall be able to find ways of describing what Flaubert is doing in *Sentimental Education*.

In the first two parts of the novel, then, he builds up a picture of a corrupt society, ripe (like the pear that symbolizes Louis-Philippe) for change. He never attempts to describe that society in a single word, but the word he most often returned to in his correspondence was 'bourgeois'. Maurice Nadeau puts it this way:

> For Flaubert, 'bourgeois' does not denote just a sociological category or a social class. For him it means anyone who thinks, feels, and acts in terms of utilitarianism, who rejects the individual in all his humanity and uniqueness in favour of the monster, society; who accepts as just and true the values this monster secretes in order to maintain its own existence as the meeting-place of all illusions, all hard-and-fast definitions of good and evil, all the commonplaces of language, stupidity in all its finery, revered and adulated under the names of

[6]'Un homme n'est jamais un individu; il vaudrait mieux l'appeler un *universel singulier*: totalisé et, par là même, universalisé par son époque, il la retotalise en se reproduisant en elle comme singularité.' *L'Idiot de la Famille*, Vol. I, p. 7.

Imp. Aubert & Cⁱᵉ.

Chez Aubert Pl. de la Bourse.

— On a dit au Gouvernement qu'il ne marchait pas, alors naturellement l'idée lui est venue de prendre tous les chemins de fer!......
— C'est vouloir aller trop vite !.......

Fig. 3 Honoré Daumier, Tout ce qu'on voudra. *'The government has been told that things weren't moving, so naturally the idea came to them of taking over all the railways.' 'That's wanting to go too fast.' (Bibliothèque Nationale)*

general truth, the 'wisdom of the nations', and the canons of morality. For Flaubert the 'bourgeois in overalls' and the 'bourgeois in a frockcoat' were the same: he hated them both as simultaneously products and promoters of a society which worshipped the Golden Calf only less than its own illusory image of itself, and which dismissed as unworthy of consideration men's individual reasons for living, creating, and dying. (Maurice Nadeau, *The Greatness of Flaubert*, Alcove Press, 1972, pp. 202–3.)

It should be noted that Flaubert's use of the word 'bourgeois' is not identical with Marx's. When Marx uses the word he refers *primarily* to a social class and a social structure, whereas to Flaubert the word indicates certain *values*.[7] Of course the two usages overlap: Marx also uses bourgeois as an adjective to refer to the values associated with the class-interests of the bourgeoisie, and Flaubert associates bourgeois values with people like the Dambreuses. But whereas the basic thing about bourgeois values to Marx was that they

[7] Frédéric, deciding to return to Paris from Fontainebleau, reproaches himself for not being in Paris with the insurrection going on: 'His indifference to the country's misfortunes had something mean and bourgeois about it' (p. 329).

emerged out of the individualist bourgeois' need to exploit people economically, what Flaubert most hated was the philistine *conformity* of a society in which bourgeois values predominated.

His literary method of presenting that society is not exactly impressionistic. A great many episodes of the most varied significance (stylistically as well as in subject-matter) are presented, sometimes through the consciousness of a single character, sometimes with apparent objectivity, sometimes through Flaubert's own obvious bias. Sometimes necessary 'background' information and documentation are provided; but sometimes the significance of an episode is not explicit at all but dependent on the conveying of a mood or emotion – experiences by one or more of the characters. Flaubert mixes 'narration' (allowing an episode to appear to present itself) with 'description' (something seen and more or less explicity summed up by the author). His method is not scientific in the usual sense; yet the structure of the novel is so self-consciously analytical, so clearly designed to juxtapose one area or situation or emotion against another within a total achieved statement (the book itself), that it is not hard to see why he himself would have rejected any decisive polarity between science and art. That is why it is not irrelevant for the historian to ask himself whether *Sentimental Education* is less 'scientific' than a work labelled 'history'.

(b) The third part of the novel, which covers the 1848–51 period (plus the final episodes in 1867), presents us with an answer to the question 'What happened to Frédéric?' and implies in a hundred indirect and scarcely perceptible ways that the answer to that question is bound up with the answer to another question, 'What happened to the revolution?' When the revolution breaks out, Frédéric is, so to speak, standing poised to consummate his relationship with Mme Arnoux. By the end of Part Three we know that the relationship and (it's not too much to say) Frédéric's life have come to nothing much, nothing fulfilled, nothing that rounds anything out into a definable pattern, no sort of unity between theory and practice.

The revolution too has come to nothing much – or, more precisely, it has come to the coup of Louis Napoleon. The forces which the revolution seemed to threaten are reinstalled. M. Dambreuse is dead and his wife has married an Englishman, but Martinon is there in their place, a senator. Hussonet is doing well. So is Cisy. And the vague hopes of the revolution, shared in their different ways by Frédéric and Deslauriers, Dussardier and Regimbart, even Pellerin, have all evaporated in muddle, confusion, treachery, disillusionment. Frédéric isn't quite like the Bourbons who forgot nothing and learned nothing: he has forgotten a good deal while learning very little.

Because the failure of the revolution and the failure of Frédéric-Deslauriers' aspirations are not explicitly or schematically related it is possible to read *Sentimental Education* without realizing how important the relationship is. But to miss this point is to miss the significance of the style and structure of the novel.

13.6 'LA VIE DE BOHÈME'

We tend today, perhaps in spite of ourselves, to see 'Bohemianism' as a factor in the social life of nineteenth-century Paris, but to see it through the romanticized light of Puccini's *La Bohème*, written in the 1890s. Puccini and his librettist had based their opera on Henri Murger's, *Scènes de la vie de Bohème*, a book of fictionalized autobiography, which itself in the 1860s looked back

Fig. 4   Gustave Courbet, The Café Andler, *(engraving). (Bibliothèque Nationale)*

somewhat nostalgically on the author's younger days of the thirties and forties. And it's by way of Murger's recollections of the student life of the Latin
quarter, hauntingly reinforced by Puccini's magic power to play on our emotions, that we tend to see *la vie de Bohème* largely in terms of the somewhat
feckless but essentially amiable and even conventional young artists, of
Mimi's tiny frozen hand, of the snow falling softly by the Barrière d'Enfer, of
Musetta's waltz song and the high jinks at the Café Momus.

The truth is more complex. Bohemianism is a significant phenomenon in
nineteenth-century society for a variety of reasons, among which are: (a) it
constituted a way of life for a significant (though never numerically very
large) proportion of the population, (b) it had socio/political implications,
and (c) it is bound up with attitudes to art, to the role of the artist in society
and the nature of the work artists produced.

Sentimental Education is a basic document of Bohemianism, even though Bohemianism is not its central subject. Not only does it give us certain 'objective'
insights into *la vie de Bohème:* it is itself in certain respects a product and
expression of the phenomenon.

T. J. Clark in his book on Courbet, *Image of the People*, makes an important
point:

> In the early days, for a few years after the 1830 revolution, Bohemia had been a
> comfortable part of the *avant-garde*, supported by doting fathers and therefore
> carefree, fashionable, unscrupulous (Gautier, Houssaye, Nerval, Roger de
> Beauvoir had been its leading lights). But that group had broken up and gone
> its separate ways, into various kinds of accommodation with the market and the
> official world of art. Bohemia, after that, was an unassimilated class, wretchedly
> poor, obdurately anti-bourgeois, living on in the absolute, outdated style of the
> 'Romantics', courting death by starvation. Nerval lived through that change in
> the definition of Bohemia, and died in madness and hunger; Journet was com-
> mitted to the Salpêtrière more than once.
>
> It was this Bohemia, this confused, indigent, shifting population, with its
> Romantic postures, that Jules Vallès tried to rescue from Murger and myth in
> his book *Les Réfractaires*, published in 1865. He tried to show the real Bohemia: a
> world of grinding poverty, of absolute refusal of bourgeois society, rather than
> the sowing of flippant wild oats. It was not an irrelevant book for Vallès the

Socialist and revolutionary to write; for Bohemia in mid nineteenth-century Paris was a real social class, a real locus of dissent. And if we want to locate it within the complex social structure of Paris, we should put it alongside not the students of the Latin quarter but the *classes dangéreuses*. It was this dangerous element – this mob of unemployed, criminals and *déclassés* of every sort, the first victims, the first debris of industrialism – which made up one part of the rebel fighting force in June 1848. The great social historian of the June Days, Rémi Gossez, closes his description of the class origins of the insurgents by saying that the last category of the rebels comprised 'social outcasts of all kinds: tramps, street-porters, organ-grinders, ragpickers, knife-grinders, tinkers, errand-boys, and all those who lived by the thousand little occupations of the streets of Paris, and also that confused, drifting mass known as *la Bohème*'. (T. J. Clark, *Image of the People*, op. cit., p. 33.)

In *Sentimental Education* the only character consistently described as a Bohemian is Hussonet. He is a Bohemian of the sort referred to by Clark as belonging to the 'early days' after 1830, a 'comfortable part of the *avant-garde*'. He is from the first something of an anachronism, a frivolous observer of changes of which he has little real comprehension, a dandy whose trendiness is somehow always a bit out of fashion, hard as he tries to keep up with the latest thing. He is cynical and unscrupulous, and his eye for the chances that come along leads him to use his circle of friends to further his own interests. He is equally prepared to exploit or reject Arnoux, Pellerin, Frédéric himself (to say nothing of the women) for his own modish, quickly-changing appetite and purposes.

Flaubert, then, in habitually referring to Hussonet as a Bohemian, is limiting his use of the word to a specific trend among people interested in art at this time and the shift of the title of the periodical *L'Art Industriel* to *L'Art* under his régime (p. 119) is significant. Hussonet has no interest in *useful* art. His 'Bohemian' view of the 1848 Revolution is several times contrasted with Frédéric's more idealized 'Romantic' view and Dussardier's more political and class-oriented view. The Bohemianism of Hussonet is characterized by an essentially frivolous view of reality:[8] he skims across the surface picking up attitudes and possibilities that happen to suit his immediate purposes. All Flaubert's scorn of the dilettante emerges in his presentation of Hussonet. If you refer back to the passage by T. J. Clark quoted above you will notice how accurately the first two sentences reflect Hussonet's position.

What emerges from *Sentimental Education* is, however, a view of *la vie de Bohème* much more profound than this portrait – excellent as it is – of one Bohemian of the older type. The remarks of Clark taken as a whole are relevant to Flaubert's novel, taken as a whole. In this connection some pages of Walter Benjamin, from his *Charles Baudelaire*, are suggestive.

Benjamin divides the history of Bohemianism into three periods: (i) the *bohème dorée* of Gautier and Nerval (Clark's 'fashionable and unscrupulous' artists of the thirties); (ii) the *bohème* of the generation of Baudelaire (essentially the forties and fifties); and (iii) the proletarianized *bohème* whose spokesman was Jean Vallès (see Clark's point about *Les Réfractaires*). You might say that *Sentimental Education*, written in the sixties, treats the first period of Bohemianism historically (through Hussonet), is deeply 'about' (without defining theoretically) the second period and is written at the time of – and therefore to some extent with a consciousness of – the third period. Benjamin discusses a passage from Baudelaire's poem, 'The Ragpickers'

---

[8]Note the sentence: 'Hussonet was in a thoughtful mood: the eccentricities of the Revolution surpassed his own' (p. 292).

Wine' (translated by C. F. MacIntyre):

> One sees a ragpicker knocking against the walls
> Paying no heed to the spies of the cops, his thralls,
> But stumbling like a poet lost in his dreams;
> He pours his heart out in stupendous schemes.

Benjamin comments:

> A ragpicker cannot, of course, be part of the *bohème*. But from the litterateur to the professional conspirator, everyone who belonged to the *bohème* could recognize a bit of himself in the ragpicker. Each person was in a more or less obscure state of revolt against society and faced a more or less precarious future. At the proper time he was able to feel with those who were shaking the foundations of this society. (Walter Benjamin, *Charles Baudelaire: A Lyric Poet in the Era of High Capitalism*, trans. Zohn, 1969 (NLB), p. 20.)

What has this discussion of *la bohème* to do with *Sentimental Education*?

Discussion

● I am not suggesting that a knowledge of the discussion of Bohemianism by such critics as Clark and Benjamin is essential to the reader of *Sentimental Education*, nor that Flaubert in his novel is consciously 'dealing with' the subject. Yet the two approaches (the one critical/historical, the other the approach to the novelist) do, it seems to me, throw light on one another.

One of the striking things about *Sentimental Education* is the sense Flaubert conveys of people cut off from their roots, drifting, experimenting, taking their pleasure and dreaming their dreams in a context within which they have little sense of 'belonging' and almost no sense of social obligation of the sort one finds for instance in a Jane Austen novel. Mme Moreau 'belongs' in Nogent, so does old Roque as long as he stays there, but the Parisians are bound together by very little except geography. They like living there precisely because it allows them a freedom based on a kind of anonymity – the anonymity of the modern large city where people live lives of crowded loneliness. This is why Frédéric's 'education' is so lacking in any sort of firm framework of value or aspiration. The more specifically 'bourgeois' characters in the novel – Roque, the Dambreuses, Oudry, Martinon – do have at least a consistent, more or less conscious pattern to their lives, a pattern based essentially on making money. But *most* of the characters are not in any full sense 'bourgeois', that is to say they aren't engaged in a systematic or whole-hearted way in the accumulation of profit and investment of wealth. It's true they become involved in 'enterprise' (Arnoux especially), lend and borrow money, make investments, gamble, try out all sorts of schemes for 'getting on' when they have the chance: but none of them is very deeply committed emotionally to such activities. Some, like Frédéric and Cisy, inherit money: but most of Frédéric's circle are either dependent on what they or their friends can earn – like Deslauriers, Dussardier, the artists and actors, the courtesans and prostitutes – or, like Regimbart, on what his wife can earn.

To this world of drifters, pleasure-lovers, kept women, artists, ineffectual intellectuals, second-level speculators and third-level politicians, Flaubert gives no name, though he gives it a location, not France, but Paris. He isn't, like Marx, a social-analyst. His whole method, however, is *provocative* in the sense that it invites the reader to define and analyse for himself. *You can only understand his book by thinking about it.*

In this context a consideration of the phenomenon of Bohemianism seems highly relevant. Such a consideration has to involve, I'd suggest, an interplay.

Thinking about Bohemianism can help us understand *Sentimental Education*: thinking about *Sentimental Education* helps us know about *la vie de Bohème*.

La vie de Bohème is a life lived outside conventionally respectable standards in a society to which the participants feel no loyalty. Whether it was, as T. J. Clark at one point says, 'a real social class' seems doubtful; but it was certainly 'a real locus of dissent'. I want you to think about (a) its social implications and (b) its relationship to the development of art, including Flaubert's art.

All societies contain eccentrics, individuals who are regarded as odd by the majority because they develop a way of life or thought which involves a degree of non-conformity, a sense of 'differentness' from the social and intellectual norms of the class to which they belong. As long as this 'differentness' doesn't much interfere with the operation of what is in general felt to be 'normal', eccentricity is usually tolerated and even, in very secure societies, respected. Nineteenth-century Bohemianism, however, was more than an eccentricity affecting a few individuals within otherwise relatively stable classes. No doubt it began like that and Flaubert's Hussonet is indeed an example of the licensed eccentric, whose eccentricities are not really much of a threat to anyone except the individuals he exploits. But Bohemianism in Paris, as Clark and Benjamin suggest, was to become something nearer to a way of life, a deliberate attempt of a sizeable group of people to *reject* and *opt out of* the dominant values of post-1830 society, to *declass* themselves. It was a *subversive* development, not so much in the sense that an effective revolutionary movement against a bourgeois-dominated society was ever likely to emerge from *la vie de Bohème*, but in the sense that any revolutionary (or simply 'anti-Establishment') developments that took place immediately attracted the sympathy of those who lived within the Bohemian fringes of Parisian society. The inhabitants of *bohème* were not revolutionaries, but they were profoundly unrespectable and, in that context, rebels.

The reactions of the characters of *Sentimental Education* to the events of February 1848, and the degree to which they participate in them, tells us a great deal about the way people living on the fringes of the Bohemian world felt about the society of their time. We shall come back to this. My immediate emphasis is on the connection between the *social* situation and the *artistic* aims of a writer like Flaubert who could seriously describe his role as that of thinker and demoralizer (see Study Guide, p. 7).

No doubt in all societies artists have tended to be classed among the eccentrics, if only because there are rather few of them and their craft by its nature involves a good deal of individual self-discipline and isolated effort. Painting a picture or writing a novel is a special kind of activity. To that extent the artist is probably always something of an oddity. But there is a qualitative distinction between this sort of unusualness and the nineteenth-century conception of the artist as – in the nature of things – odd-man-out. Not all artists before Romanticism thought of themselves as 'moralizers': but it was certainly very unusual for them to want to be 'demoralizers'. Yet writers like Flaubert and Baudelaire came to erect a whole, powerful theory of art on the basis of this negative relationship of the artist to society. Behind Flaubert's view of his role as novelist is a conception of art which has certainly not been widely held during most periods of human history: the conception of the artist as a kind of devil, producing art not for the sake of some group or class or society of men, but for the sake of art itself.

In this connection Sartre in *L'Idiot de la Famille* has some very relevant speculations and Jonathan Culler in his radio programme has some observations (based on Sartre's) which you would do well to think about: they link the significance of Bohemianism with the development of French society after

1830 and both with the nature of the attitudes to art developed by Flaubert, Baudelaire and their generation:

> . . . as potential artists they (Flaubert's generation) found themselves alienated in two ways. First, since they could not effectively live the roles of another class they must simply refuse to live bourgeois roles, simply refuse to live. In fact, it was your inability to fit into the world which proved that you were an artist. And secondly, in rejecting the bourgeoisie, the writers of this generation became alienated from their only possible audience. This is crucial because it led to an important shift in the conception of literature. For writers of the eighteenth century and of the romantic period, literature was essentially communication: one spoke to one's contemporaries about the world (and literary success meant successful communication). Flaubert's generation, writing for no audience, came to see literature as construction rather than communication; one was constructing an object rather than speaking to others. And thus one came to aim not at something relative and attainable, like communication, but at something absolute and forever unattainable, pure beauty. The artist was newly defined as someone doubly doomed to failure. Since he was an artist he couldn't succeed in the world; but as artist he must always fall short of his artistic goal.

Disengagement from the world, art for art's sake, the cult of form and beauty, are all, as Sartre would insist, political and social attitudes, the response to a given historical situation. But ironically, the very forces which led these writers to turn away from the audience of their class ensured that they would find an audience in the very class they rejected, in the professional middle classes who needed a new ideology. Industrial capitalism and the success of their own bourgeois revolution had created a situation in which the intellectual bourgeoisie could no longer adopt egalitarian rhetoric and think of man as naturally good. They needed, in order to justify and rationalize their situation, an ironic outlook which would dismiss these ideas as just so much rhetoric, unrelated to the harsh realities of life – life which demanded hard work, discipline, practicality, order. The literature of Flaubert's generation ministered to their needs by presenting a bleak world governed by an obscure and unnamed determinism, where ideals proved useless and aspirations were inevitably frustrated. *Sentimental Education* is the best example of this literature, which Sartre sees as a historical reflection of the period's ideological needs.

To be sure, Flaubert did not give the bourgeoisie exactly what they might have liked, for his irony extended to all the attitudes which they themselves might have wished to adopt. The people who frequent the Dambreuse salon do not escape Flaubert's ironic and vituperative prose. But one can see, I think, that the business men, the technocrats, the devotees of hard fact, the practical men of Flaubert's age might have been blind to the ironies aimed at them and have read *Sentimental Education* as a demonstration of how foolish it is to waste one's time, like a Frédéric Moreau, dreaming of love and happiness, instead of getting down to work and making, as they would say, a success of oneself. For Sartre, Flaubert is an accomplice of the bourgeoisie he hated because he tried to disengage from society and failed to work for a better world. His portrayal of public life and revolution in *Sentimental Education* reflects a desire to pillory all sides and to dismiss politics as if it were simply a nuisance. This sardonic alienation is a characteristic result of the experience of Flaubert's generation: a generation whose attitudes are best understood through a great novel like *Sentimental Education*. (Jonathan Culler, *Sartre on Flaubert*, Radio programme 13.)

LA SALLE DU TRÔNE AUX TUILERIES.

LE PEUPLE AUX TUILERIES !　　　THE PEOPLE IN THE TUILERIES !

La Royauté étant en fuite . . . le peuple vainqueur entra dans le Chateau désert. . . Il respecta et fit respecter les richesses qu'il renfermait, mais il réserva sa justice et son mépris pour la salle du trône qui fût dévastée
(le 24 février, 2 heures.)

The Royalty had fled away . . . The victorious people run into the deserted Chateau . . He spared & made respected all the riches contained in it but the whole of his Justice & contempt was for the hall of state which was devastated
(February 24th 2 O'c.)

New York. Published by Goupil Vibert & C.º 289 Broadway　　Paris. GOUPIL VIBERT & C.ªⁱᵉ Editeurs.　　London. Published by E. Gambart & C.º 25 Berners St. Oxford

Fig. 5 The mob invades the throne room in the Tuileries, 24 February 1848. Engraving by A. Godard from a lithograph by V. Adam and J. Arnout. (Bibliothèque Nationale)

13.7 THE NOVEL AND HISTORY

On the strength of *Sentimental Education* how would you assess Flaubert's attitude to political and social matters and the 1848 Revolution in particular? This is a question with many ramifications and both radio broadcasts (No. 4 and No. 13) contribute to it. A full treatment would involve not only an estimate of Flaubert's attitude to the Revolution of 1848–51, but also a discussion of the nature of the value of a novel like *Sentimental Education* to the historian. I do not think it would be helpful to provide some sort of 'model

30

answer' on either. So although in the course of this section I give some of my own opinions about these questions, the main use of this part of the unit should be to stimulate discussion.

One could go through the novel abstracting the occasional specific statement which seems to bear the direct assent of the author (such as the hostile reference to socialist thinkers on p. 141): but the principal way through which Flaubert's view of the revolution emerges is by *implication* (the tone of his description of certain developments) and through the overall impression which the book as a whole leaves. One should be careful about attributing to Flaubert opinions which are in fact those of his characters. At the same time it is certainly a part of his method to give the reader the opportunity to assess the worth of opinions expressed, without overt authorial comment, by the characters themselves.

For instance Frédéric watching the revolutionary events of February 1848 from the Tuileries is described as follows:

> The ardour of the crowds had infected him. He greedily breathed in the stormy air, full of the smell of gunpowder; and at the same time he trembled with the consciousness of a vast love, a sublime, all-embracing tenderness, as if the heart of all mankind were beating in his breast. (p. 292)

This is a 'straight' description. There is no reason to infer from it either that Frédéric is insincere or that Flaubert is using a word like 'sublime' with any sort of irony. Yet I think we do undoubtedly feel as we read that there is something bogus about Frédéric's sentiments. This is partly because we already know a good deal about the young man and have learned to be suspicious about his flights of enthusiasm. But it is also because of the sentences which follow the ones I have quoted, which are: 'Hussonet gave a yawn and said: "I suppose it's time I went off to educate the masses".' Now Hussonet's cynicism doesn't prove that Frédéric's reactions are superficial or insincere. But the juxtaposing of his cynical view of the revolution with Frédéric's sympathetic one does release us from the obligation of assuming that Frédéric *is* necessarily sincere. Flaubert works in this way all the time. By juxtaposing contrary views and interpretations of what is going on he makes quite clear that he doesn't ask the reader to give a special validity to any one of them. He is leaving interpretations open. It is on the basis of our total impressions and knowledge about Frédéric (or the revolution) that we have to judge him (or it).

So Flaubert is neutral? The 'objective' narrator leaving it all to the reader? Is that it?

Discussion
● No it can't be, can it? For Flaubert decides what the reader shall read, what he shall be told, what he shall know. And not just the 'facts' (as though they had an existence of their own), but the words which describe and therefore colour the facts.

So while in one sense he doesn't force his own opinions on us and appears to give us the right to make up our own mind, in another sense he guides our every response, choosing what we shall be told and how we shall be told it.

An author, like a god, may claim to be neutral on the grounds that he is 'above' the struggles he creates or recounts. But in fact he is never neutral because, as a god, he is 'above' neutrality, creating the situation within which all judgements and choices operate.

Yet the analogy between novelist and god is less than satisfactory, not only because we know very well that Flaubert isn't a god but also because we do not and cannot isolate the experience of reading *Sentimental Education* from our other experiences of the actual world, including our knowledge of nineteenth-century France. So that one factor in our assessment of Flaubert and his novel is our knowledge that it *is* a novel written in about 1867 and does emerge from a specific context of history and experience. We do not and cannot read it as though it were a complete and independent and timeless creation. In one sense we are, as we read, totally in Flaubert's hands (for the book *is* the words he writes) but at the same time we know perfectly well that Flaubert and his book are a part of a bigger world and we don't expect them to be immune to the limitations involved in being a *part* of something.

In the same way we may accept the whole force of the '*l'art pour l'art*' position and agree to agree that art is in an important sense its own justification, yet know perfectly well at the same time that *nothing* is its own justification since nothing is separate from or independent of other things and therefore can't be seen or judged or even thought of except in relation to something else.

What on earth (you may well be complaining) is he on to now? Whatever have these issues to do with the business of assessing the relationship of *Sentimental Education* to the 1848 Revolution? Have we strayed into a philosophy course?

I raise these general questions (which you may prefer to ignore) because I think it is perhaps more important to be aware of the problems and snags skulking around an apparently straightforward question like 'What was Flaubert's attitude to the 1848 Revolution?' than to be able to offer a nice straightforward 'model answer'.

Let me suggest, then, that any satisfactory answer to that question has to involve an awareness of some of the following points:

1   It is pretty clear from his correspondence and from the tone of his novel that Flaubert had an intensely critical and indeed hostile attitude to what he considered the dominant force in French society in the 1840s – the bourgeoisie (i.e. the class that controlled industry, banking and commerce) and their values and ideology. Whether he is 'unfair' to this class is a question that can be decided partly on the basis of the reader's reactions to *Sentimental Education* (if it *convinces* you it must be in some sense *true*), partly on grounds extrinsic to the novel, i.e. your overall experience of life. But the two have to gell: otherwise one or the other has something wrong with it.

2   It is also pretty clear that Flaubert had little sympathy for, and perhaps little understanding of, the working class, the 'people' or the 'mob', i.e. those who came out into the streets of Paris in 1848 and by their presence or actions precipitated the political and social changes of the time. At best these people are seen as a powerful but rather terrifying symbolic 'force' (e.g. the young man with long black hair (p. 285), the crowds on the boulevards (p. 317)).

3   It is also pretty clear that Flaubert had little use for most of the intellectuals or artists of the day. These emerge as trendy time-servers, doctrinaire cranks and Romantic dreamers. The circle in which Frédéric Moreau moves consists largely of people who are ineffectual or corrupt or both.

4   Flaubert, in other words, had plenty of opinions and plenty of prejudices. When he said, *before* he had written his novel, that the passion related in *Sentimental Education* would be, as passion was bound to be nowadays, inactive, he was prejudging his book and to that extent making it a *roman à thèse* (but

32

does any artist *not* prejudge in this way?). One of his most revealing asides about the novel is that he had thought of calling it *Les Fruits Secs (Withered Fruit)*. That is the short answer to what he thought about 1848.

A longer answer could involve the sort of consideration given by A. W. Raitt in his *Life and Letters in France: The Nineteenth Century*. Please read the following extract carefully; it begins with a passage from the novel.[9]

> The Citizen spent his days roaming the streets, tugging at his moustache, rolling his eyes, and collecting and passing on gloomy pieces of news. He had only two phrases: 'Look out, we're going to be outflanked!' and: 'Dammit all, they're pinching the Republic!' He was dissatisfied with everything, and particularly with the fact that France had not taken back her natural frontiers. The mere mention of Lamartine's name made him shrug his shoulders. He did not consider that Ledru-Rollin was 'up to dealing with the problem'; and he regarded Dupont (of the Eure) as an old fogey, Albert as an idiot, Louis Blanc as a Utopian, and Blanqui as a thoroughly dangerous character. When Frédéric asked him what they ought to have done, he took his arm in an iron grip and replied:
>
> 'Take the Rhine, that's what! Take the Rhine, dammit!'
>
> Then he inveighed against the reactionaries.
>
> They were beginning to show their hand. The sack of the castles of Neuilly and Suresnes, the fire at Les Batignollès, the riots in Lyons – every excess and every grievance was now exaggerated; and the reactionaries threw in Ledru-Rollin's circular, the forced issue of banknotes, the drop in Government stock to sixty francs, and lastly, as the final iniquity, the last straw, the supreme horror, the forty-five-centime tax. And on top of all this there was Socialism too! Although these theories were about as new as love and war, and although in the past forty years they had been discussed in enough books to fill several libraries, they still terrified the middle classes as much as a shower of meteorites, arousing the hatred which any idea produces just because it is an idea, a detestation which later redounds to its glory and ensures its superiority over its enemies, however mediocre the idea itself may be.
>
> Now property was raised to the level of Religion and became indistinguishable from God. The attacks being made on it took on the appearance of sacrilege, almost of cannibalism. In spite of the most humanitarian legislation ever passed in France, the spectre of '93 reappeared, and the sound of the guillotine made itself heard in every syllable of the word 'Republic' – although this did not prevent people from despising it for its weakness. Conscious of no longer having a master, France began to cry out in terror, like a blind man without a stick, or a child who lost its nurse. (pp. 294-5.)

L'Éducation sentimentale, which appeared in 1869, is a novel with two purposes. One is to show the high hopes and ideals of its young hero, Frédéric Moreau, and their gradual erosion until his life degenerates into empty disillusionment. The other is to describe the events that led up to the February Revolution of 1848 which deposed Louis-Philippe, the vast expectations of social and political improvement which it awakened, and their frustration in the rise of a wave of reaction which eventually resulted in the establishment of the dictatorial Second Empire. The two themes echo each other constantly throughout the work.

This passage, which is exclusively concerned with the historical situation, is placed somewhere about the middle of March 1848. The Revolution had broken out, spontaneously and unexpectedly, on 22nd February, as the result of a ban imposed by the unpopular Guizot Government on a meeting which was to have been held that day in Paris to call for reforms in the institutions of the State. Demonstrations turned into riots, and on the 23rd, Louis-Philippe tried to abdicate in favour of his grandson, but it was already too late. The mob invaded the Chamber of Deputies and compelled the Assembly to proclaim a provisional

[9]The translations in square brackets through the extract are either from the Penguin edition of the novel or by Arnold Kettle.

Government. This was formed on the 24th, with a coalition of moderate republicans including Dupont de l'Eure, Lamartine and Ledru-Rollin, and more Left-wing elements such as Louis Blanc and Albert. Louis-Philippe fled, France was declared a republic, and an immediate programme of social reform was instituted, embracing freedom of thought and expression, a democratic constitution, universal suffrage, changes in the structure of taxation, emancipation of the working classes, and ambitious schemes of work for all in national workshops. For the time being, the middle classes and the workers, united in their detestation of the July Monarchy, were animated by a common desire for social justice and political reform, and it seemed as though the Second Republic was to accomplish the foundation of true equality which neither 1789 nor 1830 had brought about.

But it was not long before dissensions split the ranks of the republicans and fear caused a change in public opinion, and it is at the moment when this is happening that Flaubert describes a meeting between his hero Frédéric and an old friend named Regimbart, whose republican opinions under the July Monarchy had earned him the nickname of 'le Citoyen'. Regimbart, eternally dissatisfied with the course of events and too much addicted to talk ever to take any effective part in them, is gloomily preoccupied with the signs of mounting reaction and with good reason fears that the Republic of his dreams will be 'escamoté' ['pinched'] and that the genuine patriots will be 'débordés' ['outflanked'].

Regimbart is one of the republicans who clamoured in vain for the Government to seek an immediate revision of the treaties of 1815 which had fixed the new frontiers of France, and his indiscriminate denigration of all the members of the provisional Government enables Flaubert to list the eminent politicians of the day. Lamartine comes first in Regimbart's catalogue of *bêtes noires*, partly because he was at that time still the popular hero of the Revolution and partly because he was, as Minister for Foreign Affairs, responsible for the pacific foreign policy which so disgusts Regimbart. Ledru-Rollin, already a left-wing deputy before 1848, was one of the key figures in the Government, since he not only occupied the vital post of Minister for the Interior but was also the only man capable of keeping the peace between the inimical factions of moderates and socialists in the Cabinet. It is because of this heavy burden that Regimbart regards him as not being 'suffisant pour le problème ['up to dealing with the problem']. As for Dupont de l'Eure (the qualifying phrase was not part of his name but was usually added – sometimes in brackets – to distinguish him from other Duponts), he was President of the Council of Ministers; although he enjoyed immense respect after a long and honourable political career, his great age (he was eighty-one) goes some way to explaining Regimbart's disdainful epithet 'vieille ganache' ['an old fogey']. The moderates having thus been dismissed as incompetent, Regimbart goes on to display equal contempt for the socialists. Louis Blanc, journalist and political theorist, was the author of a treatise on *L'Organisation du travail* and was placed by the provisional Goverment at the head of a Commission of Workers designed to ensure full and equitable employment for all: the national workshops were a modified version of his plan for State regulation of labour. It is this desire to provide work for everyone which makes Regimbart call him a 'utopiste' ['utopian']. Albert was his ally, the only working-man member of the provisional Government, whose presence there appears to have been largely symbolic and who was in any case removed and imprisoned after a socialist demonstration had invaded the Assembly on 15th May. Finally comes Auguste Blanqui, 'homme extrêmement dangéreux' ['a thoroughly dangerous character'], who in 1848 was released from the prison sentence which he had been serving for revolutionary activities against Louis-Philippe and who then set about agitating to exert extremist pressure on the provisional Government through the secret societies and political clubs in which he was very powerful.

But if Regimbart has scant regard for the leading personalities striving to guide the new-born Second Republic, he is even more scornful of 'la réaction' ['the reactionaries'], the middle-class section of the population which was soon to thwart the social reforms that had been set in motion, and to repress once again the demands of the proletariat. This property-owning class, which had originally made common cause with the workers in the Revolution, had rapidly become alarmed at the way the situation was developing, and Regimbart lists their main grievances and worries. They fall into two categories: fright at the violence of some of the disorders which had occurred during the Revolution itself, and extreme distaste for some of the steps taken by the provisional Government. First there was the pillaging of some rich private houses, notably Louis-Philippe's summer residence at Neuilly and the Rothschild castle at Suresne. Then there were cases of incendiarism during the riots, notably in the Batignolles, a northern district of Paris. In the provinces, at Lyons and elsewhere, there had been attacks on factories and outbursts of machine-breaking. Lawlessness of this kind, though infrequent in February 1848, was nevertheless a source of disquiet to the peace-loving *bourgeoisie* who feared for their own dwellings and belongings.

Moreover, certain measures taken by the provisional Government hit their pockets and aroused anxiety for the whole future of private property. For instance, on 12th March, in a circular letter sent to the regional commissioners who had been appointed to replace Louis-Philippe's prefects, Ledru-Rollin gave warning that the Government intended to pursue a firmly Left-wing policy and insisted that candidates for the coming elections should all be democrats of long standing – 'des républicains de la veille' – and not lukewarm opportunists. At the same time, a serious financial crisis was threatening the infant Republic with bankruptcy, and Government 5 per cent stock, quoted at 116 francs when the Stock Exchange closed on 23rd February, stood at only 97 francs 50 centimes when the market reopened on 7th March, and in the following days it fell swiftly, lower even than the 60 francs Flaubert mentions. The result was that many people living modestly on their investments were ruined. Various unpopular decrees were passed to palliate this state of affairs. There was a new issue of banknotes, which were not convertible into gold as they normally would have been, and on 18th March, Garnier-Pagès, newly appointed to the Ministry of Finance to succeed Goudchaux who had resigned in despair, announced that direct taxation was to be increased in the ratio of 45 centimes per franc – in other words, by 45 per cent – a step which brought forth howls of protest from the taxpayers, especially the provincial *bourgeoisie* and peasantry, who had not in any case had much to do with the setting up of the Republic, very largely a Parisian affair.

So, with commerce almost at a standstill, income from stocks and shares drastically reduced, taxation rising steeply, continual disturbances and demonstrations by workers, increasing pressure on the Government from its socialist and communist supporters, it is not surprising that the middle classes began to dread the advent of a social upheaval so momentous that they themselves would be swept away by it. That is why the principle of private property suddenly becomes sacred (Proudhon, one of the theorists of socialism, declared: 'La propriété, c'est le vol' ['Property is theft']) and why the word 'Republic', at first the symbol of progress and justice, acquired sinister overtones of the Terror of 1793. This was the situation in mid-March 1848 which was soon to lead to demonstrations by the *bourgeois* National Guard, counter-demonstrations by the workers, the election of a largely conservative assembly in April, abortive Left-wing insurrections in May and June, after which General Gavaignac took over power until the presidential elections of December. Louis-Napoleon was then elected on a vaguely traditionalist programme and carried out an increasingly authoritarian and Right-wing policy until, taking advantage of a quarrel with the Assembly, he set up a dictatorship by the *coup d'état* of 2nd December 1851, proclaiming himself Emperor the following year. Thus the Revolution which had seemed destined to reform not only the political system but also the whole structure of society ended in the establishment of a *régime* even more reactionary and tyrannical than the one it had overthrown.

If one examines the way in which Flaubert presents his information and his analysis of the state of France in March 1848, it becomes clear that he is simultaneously pursuing two aims in this passage. The first and most obvious is that of using his novel to convey a full and accurate account of the history of his times. From this point of view, Regimbart is no more than a pretext for mentioning the names of the outstanding politicians, the most important events, the dominant currents of ideas – and Flaubert has done his work well. He used in *L'Éducation sentimentale* not only his own memories of the period and the published memoirs of his friend Du Camp, but also a whole library of historical works on 1848; in April 1867 he wrote to Louis Bouilhet: 'Je bûche la Révolution de 48 avec fureur. Sais-tu combien j'ai lu et annoté de volumes depuis six semaines? Vingt-sept, mon bon' ['I'm swotting up the Revolution of 48 furiously. Do you know how many volumes I've read and annotated in the last six weeks? Twenty-seven ...'].* The outcome of this meticulous documentation is a complete and faithful picture of the period: historians of the 1848 Revolution often quote *L'Éducation sentimentale* as evidence. As a historian, Flaubert lays claim to impartiality and objectivity:

> Je ne me reconnais pas le droit d'accuser personne. Je ne crois même pas que le romancier doive exprimer son opinion sur les choses de ce monde ... Je me borne donc à exposer les choses telles qu'elles me paraissent, à exprimer ce qui me semble le vrai. Tant pis pour les conséquences. ['I do not give myself the right to accuse anyone. I do not even believe that the novelist ought to express his opinion about the affairs of this world ... I confine myself therefore to showing things as they seem to me, to expressing what seems to me to be the truth. And to hell with the consequences.']†

It is indeed true that any manual of history would give an impression of March 1848 substantially similar to that given by Flaubert.

But the second aim, more subtly insinuated, is that of making a sombre and satirical comment on the men and events of 1848, and through them, on humanity in general. Regimbart himself is a mildly ridiculous figure, talkative, mournful, hypercritical and ineffectual. Even so, the repetition of his derogatory views on the politicians of the day tends to cast discredit on them as well as on him. When he moves on to consider the dangers of reaction, the irony becomes much more marked. The fact that genuine grievances are now being exaggerated, that a new tax can be termed the height of iniquity, the last straw, the ultimate horror, that the *bourgeois* are frightened of socialism (although it is no more a novelty than the most ancient of children's games) as they would be of a shower of meteorites, that property is confused with God, that offences against it are equated with cannibalism – all that indicates on Flaubert's part a withering contempt for the *bourgeois* reactionaries which far exceeds any scepticism about the republicans. This attitude is confirmed both by what he appears to have thought in 1848 and by what he said while writing the novel. He was sufficiently hostile to the July Monarchy to attend a reformist banquet at Rouen in December 1847, but came away angry and disillusioned:

> Quelque triste opinion que l'on ait des hommes, l'amertume vous vient au cœur quand s'étalent devant vous des bêtises aussi délirantes, des stupidités aussi échevelées. ['However poor an opinion one may have of mankind, bitterness strikes one's heart when one is faced with such nonsense, such raving wild stupidity.']‡

By May 1849, he was equally disgusted with all the parties:

> Républicains, réactionnaires, rouges, bleus, tricolores, tout cela concourt d'ineptie. ['Republicans, reactionaries, reds, blues, red-white-and-blues, all unite in ineptitude.']§

And twenty years later, he forecast that 'les patriotes ne me pardonneront pas ce livre, ni les réactionnaires non plus' ['the patriots won't forgive me for this book, nor will the reactionaries.']** Even so, he detested the reactionaries more than the democrats because they were more *bourgeois*, and that, in Flaubert's eyes, was the one unforgivable sin: 'Les réactionnaires seront encore moins ménagés que les autres, car ils me semblent plus criminels'. ['The reactionaries will be spared even less than the others, for they seem to me more criminal.']††

That is why Flaubert seems momentarily to be defending socialism (with which he had in reality no great sympathy) when he talks about 'cette haine que provoque l'avènement de toute idée parce que c'est une idée, exécration dont elle tire plus tard sa gloire, et qui fait que ses ennemis sont toujours au-dessous d'elle, si médiocre qu'elle puisse être'. ['the hatred which any idea produces just because it is an idea, a detestation which later redounds to its glory and ensures

*Gustave Flaubert, *Correspondance* (Paris, Conard; 1929), vol. v, p. 293.
†Ibid., p. 396 (to George Sand, 10th August 1868).
‡To Louise Colet, December 1847, *Correspondance*, vol. II, p. 79.
§To Ernest Chevalier, 6th May 1849, ibid., p. 87.
**To George Sand, 5th July 1868, vol. v, p. 385.
††To George Sand, 10 August 1868, ibid., p. 397.

its superiority over its enemies, however mediocre the idea itself may be.'] It is his habitual hatred of the *esprit bourgeois* in all its manifestations which leads him to this outburst, and which induces him to ridicule their fear of the guillotine by referring to 'la législation la plus humaine qui fut jamais' ['the most humanitarian legislation ever passed in France']; there is no evidence that Flaubert felt any real enthusiasm for the reforms of the Second Republic. Flaubert uses comically incongruous similes to reinforce the climax of the ridicule which he heaps on middle-class France: 'La France ... se mit à crier d'effarement, comme un aveugle sans bâton, comme un marmot qui a perdu sa bonne'. ['France began to cry out in terror, like a blind man without a stick, or a child who has lost its nurse.'] In his pessimistic view of human nature, men lack the necessary intelligence to govern themselves, their affairs are consequently ruled by chance and by the least noble of their feelings, and ideas are the last things to affect their conduct.

The question remains how Flaubert manages to preserve a pretence of objectivity and yet work up to a paroxysm of ironic indignation at the end of the last paragraph. The key lies in his cunning use of indirect speech. Nominally, he is merely reporting Regimbart's opinions, for which as an author he bears no personal responsibility, and the 'Citoyen' is briefly and rather ludicrously evoked at the outset, 'tirant sa moustache, roulant des yeux' ['tugging at his moustache, rolling his eyes'.] Moreover, some of his remarks are given in direct speech, so that one is at first keenly aware of his presence. Then he goes on to charges against the reactionaries, and these are summaries, as one would expect, in the imperfect. But half-way through the paragraph, the tense changes without warning: 'Elles épouvantèrent les bourgeois' ['They still terrified the middle classes']; a present tense intervenes as Flaubert generalises, and the remainder of the narration continues in the past definite. Once Flaubert drops the imperfect in favour of the past definite, he is speaking in his own name and not in Regimbart's, since the past definite cannot be used for reported speech. The end of the paragraph thus represents what Flaubert thinks and not what Regimbart says. In other words, he has just used Regimbart as a cover and has discarded him once he had served his purpose of disguising the introduction of Flaubert's own views. So the canon of historical objectivity and of literary impersonality which Flaubert preaches is really a way of masking the author's presence and not a way of eliminating it. He is vibrantly and vitally concerned here, full of vituperative scorn and blistering sarcasm.

The passage shows not only how the reproduction of thoroughly documented historical reality has become an integral part of novel-writing; it also reveals some of the secrets of a master-stylist who feels strongly and deeply but who believes that in his novels facts should speak for themselves (or at least should appear to do so) and who succeeds admirably in effacing himself behind his characters. Flaubert as a man, and 1848 as historical fact, are inseparable in this passage as they are throughout *L'Éducation sentimentale*, and one cannot understand the one without the other. (A. W. Raitt, *Life and Letters in France: The Nineteenth Century*, Nelson, 1965, pp. 76–82.)

A. W. Raitt's interesting examination of this passage seems to me to do two things: (a) to demonstrate the close relationship of *Sentimental Education*, which is fiction (and therefore in a certain sense not 'true'), to the actual historical situation which Flaubert is coming to grips with, and (b) to raise some interesting general questions about the status of this, and perhaps any successful, novel as history.

This last is a big question and we shall not have the time to pursue it in depth: but it is so relevant to these units that I would ask you to pause to consider one of the basic questions A. W. Raitt raises.

He argues that Flaubert has two aims in this passage, and in general: (i) 'to convey a full and accurate account of the history of his times', and (ii) to make 'a sombre and satirical comment on the men and events of 1848 and, through them on humanity in general'. But he then goes on to suggest that Flaubert's claims to objectivity are in fact a pretence and that 'the canon of historical

objectivity and literary impersonality which Flaubert preaches is really a way of masking the author's presence and not a way of eliminating it'.

The question which seems to me to need consideration here is: while it is clear that Flaubert's novel expresses *his* consciousness and indeed cannot be understood except in relation to Flaubert, *is this not also true of all works of history?* Dr Raitt writes of Flaubert 'using' a character like Regimbart as a 'cover'. Since a novelist inevitably 'uses' *all* his characters in some sense (for they do not do anything but what he makes them do), is not the important distinction between those characters which are or are not *convincing* rather than between those which are or are not *used?* Is Regimbart a convincing character? If he is, is there any more point in referring to him as a 'cover' than in describing any historian's presentation of any real character in history as a 'cover' for *his* prejudices?

I would agree, of course, that one does sometimes have the sense, in reading a novel, of a character ceasing to be convincing because he simply becomes, inappropriately, the mouthpiece of some ideas the author wishes to get across. But this is not, I believe, the phenomenon Dr Raitt is referring to. What he points out is that at a certain stage in the narrative the point of view shifts and suddenly it is Flaubert and not Regimbart speaking. This involves a manipulation of the reader's responses, but doesn't undermine the credibility of Regimbart. Regimbart in fact is being 'used' only in the sense that he must, like every character in any novel, play the part he has to play in the total conception of the novel.

It is certainly true that Flaubert, who had plenty of prejudices, can never eliminate them from the novel. This is, almost by definition, true of all the work of all artists. But in what sense is it *not* true of a historian? And do we not in the end use the same criterion to assess a novel like *Sentimental Education* and, say, Marx's account of the Revolution of 1848, that is to say its overall convincingness? The ways we test the convincingness of a work of art and that of a work of history are clearly in one sense not quite the same (you cannot ask whether there is any evidence that Regimbart actually said what he did):[10] but can there really be some final 'canon of historical objectivity' which puts the activity of the historian in a totally different category from that of the novelist?

Flaubert certainly had a view of the Revolution of 1848. It is a view most fully expressed not in his biography or correspondence but in *Sentimental Education*.[11] We know from reading *Sentimental Education* that he must have had a poor opinion of most of the people and forces and movements involved in the public events which come into his novel. It is indeed a characteristic of the whole theory of *'l'art pour l'art'* which he adopted that the artist is a very superior being who alone is able to offer some sort of absolute 'truth'. Flaubert did not think of himself as an active participant in the revolution: if he had done so he would no doubt have written differently, more modestly and with more sense of the practical possibilities of the situation he evokes. Had he been a writer committed to some specific and therefore limited and relative aim or cause he would have conceived his novel in entirely different terms and no-one can say whether it would have been better or worse.

[10]Clive Emsley makes the point that no historian would dare ask his readers to accept as convincing as long a pregnancy as Rosanette's.

[11]And because *Sentimental Education* is a novel and not an historical essay, Flaubert's personal views are mediated by the very form (the novel) which he uses to express them and you can't properly discuss his views *except* as they are mediated through his novel.

The problem about asking a question like 'Is Flaubert fair to the revolutionaries? or 'Is he sufficiently objective about the bourgeoisie?' is that it may lead you, in considering what Flaubert did not do or might perhaps have done, to fail to recognize what he did do. For myself, I certainly don't think I get from *Sentimental Education* much sense of the nature and aspirations of 'the mob' (though one gets some vivid images of it, all coloured by a more or less hostile attitude). It doesn't worry me very much that Flaubert's attitude to life and politics, especially when abstracted from his novels, seems unsatisfactory – superior and cynical and neurotic. I don't feel called upon to *agree* with the view of life and history implicit in *Sentimental Education*. I don't put down the book feeling that I've been given the key to a door which, unlocked, will reveal a short cut to truth and happiness. But I do find the novel continuously revelatory, not least of the dilemmas of Flaubert himself whose art itself emerges as a defining factor of the situation he writes about. If there is something extraordinarily 'objective' about *Sentimental Education* this comes, I'd suggest, not from any absence of prejudice or partiality, not from an ability to get 'beyond' the limitations of a class or its ideology, but from the clarity with which prejudice and limitations are revealed. Flaubert may have persuaded himself that as an artist he was 'above' all struggles; but what, amid much else, he has to offer the historian is one of the most potent revelations in literature that no-one, neither artist nor historian, is.

APPENDIX: 'SCARLET AND BLACK' AND 'SENTIMENTAL EDUCATION' (Chiefly for those who read Stendhal's *Scarlet and Black* for *The Age of Revolutions* Course[12])

Stendhal's *Scarlet and Black*, written in the years just preceding the 1830 revolution, could well be thought of as a 'sentimental education' of its day. It is the story of a young man confronting his destiny. In the telling of the story, private and public worlds, love and politics, continuously interact. Like Flaubert's book it is, in a very basic sense, an historical novel, the history of a generation. It is also a novel about social revolution. As Frédéric Moreau is a child of the revolution of 1830, of the bourgeois monarchy of Louis Philippe, so is Julien Sorel a child of the 1789 revolution and of the Napoleonic wars. Both novelists begin with a post-revolutionary situation of which their respective heroes are the products. Both view the young men's lives in the light of a changing world.

Neither Julien nor Frédéric is, in the triter sense of the word, heroic. Julien, the son of a peasant, is deeply conscious of his need to make his way in an unfamiliar and in many respects hostile world. He has nothing to help him except his intelligence, good looks and, behind him, a revolution full of promises for a young man with his eye on the future. He sets about systematically to educate himself, improve his social position, and increase his power *vis-à-vis* the world he has been born into. In these aims he is remarkably successful. Whether as tutor in a provincial bourgeois household, as an abbé in a seminary, or as secretary to a politically-minded aristocrat, he is a highly successful operator, worming his way into positions of power, partly with the help of (and partly with the aim of winning sexually) the wife and daughter of successive employers.

Compared with Julien, Frédéric is a pretty ineffectual figure. He has no need to work hard for *his* fortune and is happy enough to live on an unearned income. And though he is no less involved with other people's wives and

[12]The Open University, (1972) A202 *The Age of Revolutions*, The Open University Press.

mistresses, his sexual life isn't precisely triumphant. Why, then, do I press the comparison between them?

Largely because the differences between the novels – themselves historically based – seem to throw a good deal of light on each other and on French history of the nineteenth century. These differences do not consist simply in their subject-matter, what they are *about*; but – more interestingly – in what they *are*, their significance as literary texts or offerings in the changing world of France between 1789 and 1867.

Stendhal's novel, in style or form as well as content, is above all an expression of the liberating force of the French Revolution. What gives Julien Sorel his energy, not simply as a 'character' or 'force' but as an artistic creation, is the way in which he embodies certain human aspirations released by the Revolution of 1789. These aspirations – towards a fuller freedom of choice and development, both personal and social – are not expressed in idealistic or abstract terms. Julien is not, by most standards either of his time or ours, a very admirable young man. He is egocentric and unscrupulous and a lot of the time he doesn't know at all clearly what he wants or why but is driven on by an effort of will which he scarcely understands and which lands him in appalling situations and difficulties. Most important, perhaps, he is a sort of embodiment of Romantic aspiration, for good and for bad.

Stendhal himself was not a part of the French Romantic movement. The spirit behind his work is rational, dialectical, hard-headed, critical, urbane. Yet he would never align himself *against* the Romantics and would insist that at each stage of cultural and literary development the new and vital literature of the day would be Romantic in spirit. Romanticism for him meant the expression of the changing values and new human possibilities generated by the social development of the time. He did not *identify* with the forces of Romanticism in the way a writer like Victor Hugo did, but he *expressed* them through a literary art which stressed the paradoxes, contradictions, and conflicts of the situations he presented. Julien Sorel is presented, for most of *Scarlet and Black*, not from the inside but objectively as an energetic but disturbing force confronting the existing forces of inertia, prejudice and established interests. Stendhal's method is to present his reader with situations of conflict in which Julien is involved and then, without our quite realizing it, to inject the question: 'Where do your sympathies lie?' And the answer is always: 'That depends which side you are on'. Whether you consider Julien an intolerably ungrateful and immoral upstart or a young man asserting his right to fulfilment depends on whether you are a partisan of the old order or of the French Revolution. Stendhal does not draw a veil over the unpleasing qualities of his hero but he allows us to feel the full human impact of his aspiration for a greater measure of freedom and sincerity (and, as a corollary, a more active part in the control of the society that contains him).

This strategy reaches its climax in the final chapters of *Scarlet and Black* in which Julien faces execution for the attempted murder of his mistress, Mme de Rênal. In these remarkable pages the full force of the young peasant's claims as Romantic hero is exposed. Julien undertakes a self-examination of the greatest intellectual and emotional energy and achieves an objectivity about himself which not only establishes once for all his *bona fides* as hero but ironically 'places' the false romanticization of him by Mme de Rênal's rival, Mlle de la Mole. We are assured by the end of the novel that the quality of the relationship between Julien and Mme de Rênal is, in a quite unsentimental way, its own justification. Julien's energy, which is the energy of the French Revolution, has succeeded – whatever his personal weaknesses and errors and whether you like it or not – in establishing itself as an objective force of the greatest human potential. So that *Scarlet and Black* – a work which breathes the spirit of the Enlightenment and the Code Napoleon rather than what we most easily associate with Romanticism – emerges as an extraordinary statement of the power of Romantic ideas in pre-1830 France. Julien has found in his journey through Romanticism the strength to face life and death realistically. In this journey an essential part is played by the figure of the first Napoleon. He is always close to the young man's thoughts, a symbol of his own aspirations and of the possibility of fulfilling them. It isn't too much to say that it is above all from the symbolic example of Napoleon as a carrier of the message of the revolution that Julien's Romantic strength receives its most basic inspiration. Stendhal himself was a liberal Bonapartist to whom Napoleon personified all that was most virile in Romanticism.

With Frédéric it is all very different. Flaubert's young man, his head stuffed with Romantic attitudes, uses them only to reconcile himself, not very successfully, to his own impotence. The contrast between him and Julien is not however basically a matter of character, for the two young men's 'characters' are themselves, in a very fundamental sense, the changing products of two contrasted historical situations. The same Romantic ideas which in the eighteen-twenties Stendhal reveals as a source of strength and liberation to the peasant-intellectual Julien, Flaubert (looking at the late forties with the hindsight of the sixties) sees as useless – and indeed a source of enervating weakness – to the petty-bourgeois-intellectual Frédéric. The ladder that takes the scared and naïve but basically confident Julien to Mme de Rênal's bedroom is replaced by Frédéric's retreat from the brothel at Nogent and Mme Arnoux's failure to turn up to her critical assignation[13]; and Frédéric goes on retreating all his life. As Maurice Nadeau puts it:

> The generation of 1820, their ears ringing with the loud exhortations of Romanticism, were reduced (by the 1840s) to inaction, confronted with a mean and cramping reality. Unable to live their dreams, they settled for dreaming their lives. Frédéric is the incarnation of this generation and his behaviour is typical, almost symbolic. (Nadeau, op. cit., p. 180.)

Is it possible to make more precise the phrases 'loud exhortations of Romanticism' and 'mean and cramping reality'? Only, I suspect, by a fuller examination of the history of nineteenth-century France than we have here the space for. The sort of 'exhortations of Romanticism' (of Rousseau and Wordsworth, Shelley and Byron) Nadeau refers to involved above all a determination to give a concrete reality to the slogan 'Liberty, Equality, Fraternity'. Romanticism cannot be equated with a furtherance of radical politics (Romantics like Scott and Chateaubriant – or the later Wordsworth – were not political radicals at all): but the two meet in the element of *individual* liberation and extended aspiration characteristic of all Romantic art. Julien Sorel's relationship with Mme de Rênal, his battle against the Jesuits, his attempts to give the word sincerity a firmer foundation, his rejection of the petty-bourgeois values of his friend Fouqué and of the romantic-feudal ones of Mathilde de la Mole, all these are part and parcel of an effort to live sincerely, i.e. to achieve a realistic, active and humanly satisfying participation in the world into which he is born. Julien is at first ambitious in an instinctive way, posing his ego and cunning against the world of the Restoration, the bourgeois monarchy of the 1830–48 period, in order to be absorbed into it. But by the end of the novel he is no longer ambitious in the individualist sense: participation has come to mean an acceptance of a more objective reality, a scheme of values that is no longer that of bourgeois individualism. If Julien, in the end, virtually commits suicide, his death is an act of courage and integrity which in its Romantic way illuminates both the sordid cynicism of his enemies and the value he himself has placed on a new level of sincerity. That is why I have

---

[13]Interestingly both ladies are 'tested' by sick children.

described *Scarlet and Black* as a novel in which the spirit of Romanticism is able to lead to the achievement of a new and dynamic realism.

Flaubert's Frédéric achieves no such breakthrough. The furthest his consciousness can reach is to a rather shame-faced and cynical acceptance of his own ineffectuality and a nostalgia for lost innocence. In Flaubert's world there is no force that can help a young man towards a realistic sincerity in which values are no longer subservient to the corrupting power of things as they are. Bonapartism has changed from the progressive force that inspired Julien (even if it led him to his death) to a reactionary one which can inspire only those whom a Julien most despises. To Flaubert, dedicated to his hatred of the bourgeois world, the bourgeois world is invincible: the Romantic breakthrough is merely a self-indulgent delusion.

If you are interested in history the sort of problems these novels pose are:

Why, by 1867 (as opposed to 1830) did Romanticism no longer seem to be a possible breakthrough for a writer like Flaubert seeking to extend realism?

Had the momentum of the Revolution of 1789, which could still in the late twenties provide an impetus for Stendhal's more optimistic exploration of the 'human situation' in nineteenth-century France, really disappeared by 1851, as Flaubert implies?

Is Sartre right in seeing Flaubert's obsession with *'l'art pour l'art'* as a form of capitulation to bourgeois society?

What light does the reading of great novels throw on the history of nineteenth-century France?

ACKNOWLEDGEMENT

Grateful acknowledgement is made to the author for the extract from A. W. Raitt, *Life and Letters in France in the Nineteenth Century*, Nelson.

Notes

Notes

Notes

Notes

THE REVOLUTIONS OF 1848

Part I   **Unit 1**   Introduction to the study of revolutions and some interpretations of 1848
Unit 2   Europe on the eve of 1848
Unit 3   Document collection
Unit 4   *Sentimental Education*: a Study Guide

Part II   **France 1848–1851**
Unit 5   France, February–December 1848
Unit 6   France, January 1849–December 1851
Unit 7   Interpretation of the French Revolution: Karl Marx and Alexis de Tocqueville
Unit 8   Art in the French Revolution

Part III   **Germany, Austria and Italy**
Unit 9   Revolutions in Germany
Unit 10   Revolutions in the Austrian Empire
Unit 11   Revolutions in Italy
Unit 12   Music and revolution: Verdi

Part IV   **Unit 13**   Flaubert's *Sentimental Education*
Unit 14 } Britain and Ireland in the 1840s
Unit 15 }
Unit 16   Surveys and themes